Advance P [barcode] D0255471

Worship on ... .

"Through the complex lens of worship, Yee adds texture and depth to our understanding of Asian cultures that grace North America and suggests ways for the majority culture to engage their Asian neighbors in the faith, adding clarity to how Asian perspectives on Christianity can enrich worship for all. The author's experience as a pastor and professor and the book's organization and clear writing style make this volume equally accessible for seminarians and congregations who want to understand what it means to worship more fully in the twenty-first century."

—C. Michael Hawn, DMA, University Distinguished Professor of Church Music Director Sacred Music Program, Perkins School of Theology, Southern Methodist University, Dallas, Texas

"Christians across the Asian American spectrum will be inspired to be more intentional about asking what it means to be authentically Asian in their service of God. Russell Yee is to be thanked for these eminently challenging but no less encouraging and edifying words that portray possibilities for Asian American Christianity."

—Amos Yong, J. Rodman Williams Professor of Theology, Regent University School of Divinity, Virginia Beach, Virginia

"If we accept Russell Yee's apropos comparison of Asian North American Christian worship to a teenager, then Russell would be the caring relative who goes out of his way to share words of wisdom. *Worship on the Way* is an invaluable resource for anyone looking to connect one's God-given identity with worship to the One 'from whom all blessings flow.'"

—S. Edward Yang, Associate Director, ISAAC
(Institute for the Study of Asian American Christianity),
PhD Candidate, Fuller Theological Seminary

"Russell Yee has identified a need for a uniquely Asian North American worship tradition that fully expresses ANA ethnicity and identity. *Worship on the Way* lays a strong foundation for the development of such a tradition. Yee's contribution is clearly thought out, theologically engaging, and scripturally centered. The worship resources in Part Two of the book will provide a valuable resource for ANA church musicians, pastors, and theologians. This book should be read by anyone seeking to create a theological foundation for culturally contextualized worship."

—Brad Berglund, author of *Reinventing Sunday* and *Reinventing Worship*

Worship
on the Way

Exploring
Asian
North American
Christian
Experience

Russell Yee

Foreword by John D. Witvliet

JUDSON PRESS
PUBLISHERS SINCE 1824

Join our mailing list for updates and special offers.
www.judsonpress.com/mailing_list.cfm

For Lisa, and our Julia and Erica

Worship on the Way
Exploring Asian North American Christian Experience

© 2012 by Judson Press, Valley Forge, PA 19482-0851
All rights reserved.

Unless otherwise noted, Bible quotations in this volume are from the New Revised Standard Version of the Bible, copyright © 1989 by the Division of Christian Education of the National Council of the Churches of Christ in the United States of America. Used by permission. All rights reserved.

Bible quotations marked NIV are from the HOLY BIBLE, NEW INTERNATIONAL VERSION®. NIV®. Copyright © 1973, 1978, 1984, 2011 by Biblica, Inc.™ Used by permission. All rights reserved worldwide.

Interior and cover design by Wendy Ronga, Hampton Design Group.

Library of Congress Cataloging-in-Publication Data
Yee, Russell.
Worship on the way: exploring Asian North American Christian experience/ Russell Yee; foreword by John D. Witvliet.—1st ed. p. cm.
ISBN 978-0-8170-1707-1 (pbk.: alk. paper) 1. Asian Americans—Religion. 2. Asians—Canada—Religion. 3. Worship. 4. Asian American churches. I. Title. BR563.A82Y44 2012
264.0089'9507—dc23   2011047857

Printed in the U.S.A.
First Edition, 2012.

Foreword

Many of you may have picked up this book because you are Asian North American. You may be a first-generation immigrant or second, or somewhere in between. You may be a pastor, ministry leader, or congregational member. Others of you may have picked up this book even though you are not Asian North American. Perhaps you are married to someone who is. Perhaps you attend a church with a significant number of members of Asian descent. Perhaps you serve in a ministry that works closely with Asian North American congregations.

These audiences are different. But these audiences are also interlinked and interdependent.

They (we!) are all *interlinked* in that we are a part of Christ's body, the church, which spans cultures and centuries. What happens to one part of us affects all of us. Blessed are the readers and congregations that study this book in spite of, and not just because, of their own daily interaction with Asian communities! For everyone who reads this book will be given questions and insights to help us understand more deeply the cultural dynamics that shape all of us.

We are also *interdependent*. We need one another in order for our learning about culture, ethnicity, and Christian practice to have poise and balance. Russell Yee recognizes that without genuine intercultural learning, none of us has the perspective necessary for accurate self-assessment. We become trapped in our own inevitably limited perspective.

This means that one of the best ways to reflect on the material presented here is to read it in community, and preferably in more than one kind of community—in ethnically homogenous communities and in pan-Asian communities, in multicultural communities and in communities with common experiences of immigration. Intercultural learning best happens by experiencing it in intentionally shaped learning conversations.

This kind of integrated learning is important because questions about Christianity and culture are notoriously difficult to address. At times, the very same Christian community can be resisting cultural adaptation in one area of its life, while adopting other forms of adaptation without even thinking about it.

The reason we face these challenges is nothing less than the incarnation of Jesus Christ. The confession that the Word became flesh and lived among us—as a person in a particular time, place, and culture—is the confession that grounds and inspires our cultural engagement. What a privilege to struggle together so that the church, the body of Christ, may, live and move within particular cultural contexts with grace and truth.

Russell Yee's vision is not merely that we would study, talk, and learn together. Yee challenges us to rise up as adopted brothers and sisters in God's growing family, expressing our identity in and through acts of common worship. Ultimately, the book leads us to prayer, to proclamation of God's Word, and to feasting together around the Lord's Table.

May the Holy Spirit grant us the capacity to discern the most fruitful ways of affirming our cultures, of challenging our cultures, and of sharing together across cultures. May all of this find deep expression in worship life across the spectrum of North American Christianity and beyond.

John D. Witvliet
Calvin College and Calvin Theological Seminary
Calvin Institute of Christian Worship
Grand Rapids, Michigan

Preface

It has been more than ten years since the Pacific Asian American Canadian Christian Education (PAACCE), a working group of the Education Leadership Ministries Commission (ELMC) of the National Council of Churches-USA initiated the idea that became this book.

During the early years of PAACCE, we thought it would be a simple process of collecting suitable worship materials from Asian North American (ANA) churches and presenting them in book form. We discovered that the greater need is actually first to make a case for the need for ANA worship by providing education and inspiration around even the most basic questions: "Does culture *really* matter?" "What does being ANA have to do with how we worship?" "Why can't we all just worship the Christian way?"

This book starts with such "from scratch" ANA worship materials, with the hope of sparking the kind of fresh creativity and efforts that will someday make for a full collection. *Liturgy* is the work of the people, after all, and we hope this seminal book will inspire ANA churches to rediscover and drink from the wells of their peoples' culture, traditions, and values in ways that will enhance and enliven worship experience.

In 2004 the PAACCE group participated in the *Crossings* worship renewal conference at the American Baptist Seminary of the West in Berkeley, California. (See chapter 6, "Explorations.") There we met Russell Yee, who had conceived, organized, and led that event. We were impressed by his passion for worship generally and for matters of worship and culture specifically. It was such an ambitiously envisioned conference, clearly motivated by Yee's longing for an ANA voice in worship. We decided to recruit him for this project, and he readily accepted.

During the long development process that followed, two things changed to make this a different book than it would have been a decade ago. The first is the rise of the World Wide Web, which makes it vastly easier to find and share images, texts, audio, and video for worship, all without needing a book. For this reason, this volume has a companion website, worshipon-theway.blogspot.com. The second major change has been the rapid development of churches from newer Asian immigrant groups, especially from Southeast Asia. Ten years ago our project might have focused exclusively on East Asian groups that have been here many generations. Instead, this book tries to give substantial attention to more recent arrivals, including a whole chapter (chapter 9, "Another Beginning") about churches among the various people groups from Burma.

As a group committed to the advocacy of Christian education and leadership resources, PAACCE is pleased to place this book in your hands. May it answer questions you have been asking as well as raise new ones for you. Please help us by introducing the book to your faith communities and by disseminating the information as widely as you can. May it open new seasons of life-giving worship for your churches, and may God use it to build something beautiful and true for the ANA church and for the world.

Rev. Dr. Winfred B. Vergara
President, PAACCE
& Missioner for Asiamerica Ministries
The Episcopal Church Center

Acknowledgments

I would like to thank the Pacific Asian American Canadian Christian Education committee (PAACCE), which initiated and sponsored this project and kept it alive through a vastly longer process of development than anyone expected. Its members encouraged me at every turn and always believed in the worth of this project. I would especially like to thank Garland Pierce, formerly on staff with the National Council of Churches and now with the World Council of Churches, whose persistence, capabilities, and goodwill while serving with PAACCE bridged some of the most needful final stretches towards publication. I would also like to thank my editor at Judson Press, Rebecca Irwin-Diehl, whose skillful direction and advice shaped and improved this book in very many ways.

I owe a debt of gratitude to all my friends at New Life Christian Fellowship in Castro Valley, California, where I was pastor for ten years. Together we explored ways to express Asian American Christian culture and identity in visual art, sermon illustrations, music, and approaches to outreach. I owe a similar debt of gratitude to New Hope Covenant Church in Oakland, California, where I currently serve and worship and where I have explored all these matters further, especially pressing into the world of Southeast Asian North America. My thanks also to Tim Tseng, under whose leadership at what became the Institute for the Study of Asian American Christianity (ISAAC) I developed many of the early ideas for this book, especially through our collaborations on the "Waterwind" (2003) and "Crossings" (2004) events at the American Baptist Seminary of the West

(ABSW). Likewise, I would like to thank the Calvin Institute of Christian Worship and especially its Worship Renewal Grants Director, Betty Grit. Most of the projects I describe in Chapter 6 were made possible by Calvin Worship Renewal Grants. Betty was an unfailing support, encouragement, guide, and inspiration through each and every project. Finally, to my many former students at ABSW, at Fuller Seminary Northern California, at Logos Evangelical Seminary, and elsewhere, I give thanks for their attention and interest in exploring these topics together.

Introduction

Do you identify with Asian North American (ANA) culture, whether by your own ancestry, your relationships, where you live, or your experiences through education, work, or ministry? If so, let me ask you a question—a question that has to do with your identity in Christ, with your faith journey, with your calling and witness in the world, and maybe even with some dimensions of your experience of the new heaven and new earth.

Here's the question: If you wanted to find particularly full and deep expressions of ANA identity and culture, where would you go? Where would be some good places to encounter the ANA experience and journey in meaningful and life-giving ways?

Would you go to a wedding banquet filled with special foods, tradition-filled ways of dressing, and celebration customs passed on from generation to generation? Would you visit an Asian art or history museum? Would you turn to works from the dramatically growing body of ANA writers, artists, filmmakers, architects, and musicians? Would you survey the research and learning done at one of the more than 140 ANA departments on university and college campuses? Would you catch a street festival, parade, or even just a meal in any of ANA enclaves in our cities—Chinatowns, K-Towns, J-Towns, Little Cambodias, Little Saigons, or Little Manilas? Would you trace the entrepreneurial endeavors of ANA businesses, from mom-and-pop stores to high-tech industries, from creative design firms to professional offices? Would you profile the myriad ANA community organizations such as health clinics, cultural centers, and immigrant advocacy organizations? Would you campaign for an

ANA political candidate or track the career of ANA appointed high officials? Would you surf through the vastly proliferating array of ANA-themed blogs, video threads, and websites? Would you cheer on an ANA superathlete?

These are all important expressions of ANA culture and vital facets of ANA aspiration, creativity, adaptation, and influence. We can be thankful for such an inspiring range of ANA life and ongoing accomplishment.

Unfortunately, one of the places you are not likely to seek a particularly full and deep expression of ANA identity and culture is an ANA Christian church. Whether you visit a bilingual congregation with many first-generation immigrants or visit an all-English-speaking congregation specializing in creative, next-generation forms of multicultural ministry, by and large you will find forms of worship that are more closely tied to the majority culture than to anything identifiably ANA. The many aspects of identity and culture that are worthy of care and attention outside our churches often seem quite removed from what we do inside our churches on Sunday mornings—except perhaps at a church potluck lunch.

What does it mean to worship and serve Jesus as an ANA believer? How do matters of ancestry, culture, identity, and heritage shape the faith journeys and worship lives of ANA Christians? What might ANA believers themselves and the church worldwide be missing if the intersection of Christian worship and ANA identity and culture remains largely unexplored and undeveloped?

Worship on the Way

"The Way" is the oldest name we have on record for what we today think of as Christianity. It is what the earliest followers of Jesus first called themselves (Acts 9:2), this some time before the term *Christian* was coined (Acts 11:26). We do not know who came up with this name "the Way" or why, although we may guess that it emerged from Jesus' teaching about himself as the way, truth, and life (John 14:6). From the very beginning, Jesus' followers ultimately put their faith not in his teachings or even his actions, but in his person. To "belong to the Way" was not to belong to an organization, movement, or philosophy, but rather to a person: Jesus, the Way.

But there is another very striking text about Jesus being the Way—a text for which ANA culture can provide an especially helpful perspective.

English versions of John 1:1 usually translate the Greek *logos* as "word": "In the beginning was the Word, and the Word was with God, and the Word was God." This use of "word" to translate *logos* is technically accurate but not very evocative. Unlike "word," the Greek *logos* was not just a grammatical term or a reference to things that today we find in a dictionary. *Logos* was a philosophical term for something that gave the world its underlying order and meaning.

While every "word" in a dictionary is as much a word as any other, *logos* referred to especially clear and well-reasoned speech that reflected the true nature of the world. Why do the heavens and earth continue on as they do? How do the tiniest creatures and also the stars and planets arrange themselves harmoniously? What is it that keeps constant the meanings of light and darkness, order and chaos, and life and death? How do all these opposite forces somehow stay balanced age after age? What are truth and beauty, and why do we recognize them and long for them? It is because of the *logos*.

In Chinese translations of the Bible, *logos* is usually translated "*Tao*." This word can mean a literal road, way, or path; figuratively, it can mean a method or principle. In Taoism, the Tao is the way of all things, the underlying first principle of the universe, the reason everything has a place and order that fits everything else. To live in harmony with the Tao is to live in harmony with the forces that keep the universe balanced. To live in disharmony with the Tao is to be subject to a painful and ultimately losing battle with rebalancing forces.

Although the Tao is not a personal being, it is in the realm of philosophical possibility to say, "In the beginning was the Tao." However, to say, "the Tao became flesh and dwelled among us" would be utterly preposterous. The first principle of Taoism is that *the Tao one can speak of is not the true Tao*. In other words, the Tao lies so far beneath everything in the universe that even to speak of it is to be in the realm of secondary and later things. Perforce, anything one can touch, see, and have a personal relationship with is surely not the true Tao.

And yet this is precisely the central and astonishing claim of Christianity: that God became flesh and dwelled among us. All religions and all belief systems are ways to try to understand the world as we see it and our lives as we must live them. To believe that the universe has some kind of order and meaning is part of what makes us human. The idea of the Tao (like the idea of the *logos*) is one way to try to understand that order and meaning. Christianity takes that same longing for order and meaning and—amazingly—finds them in a person, the person described in texts such as these:

> For in him all things in heaven and on earth were created, things visible and invisible, whether thrones or dominions or rulers or powers—all things have been created through him and for him. He himself is before all things, and in him all things hold together. (Colossians 1:16-17)

> "I am the Alpha and the Omega, the first and the last, the beginning and the end." (Revelation 22:13)

> In the beginning was the Word, and the Word was with God, and the Word was God. (John 1:1)

So we have a movement called the Way, and a person who claims to be the Way. We have the Greek idea of the *logos* and the Eastern idea of the Tao. And they all come together in the person of Jesus Christ. To "worship on the way" is both to be a worshipper on the Christian journey as well as to be on that journey fully with and for the one who is the Way.

This book follows the 1996 collection of essays edited by the late David Ng, *People on the Way: Asian North Americans Discovering Christ, Culture, and Community* (Valley Forge: Judson Press). That anthology explored a wide range of ANA Christian topics, case studies, and issues. Since then, the ANA church landscape has changed in some ways. There are many new churches and a shift in some ANA circles to move to a multiracial/multicultural identity and sensibility. The small body of literature on the ANA church is growing. But some things have not changed. Immigration continues at high rates for numerous ANA people groups. Bilingual congregations and ministries continue to dominate the overall ANA landscape. Seminary-based faculty, programs, and resources specifically directed at ANA leadership and ministry remain painfully few. Questions of how to culturally contextualize worship, spirituality, evangelism, discipleship, and ministry remain as open as ever, particularly in the more evangelical-leaning congregations that dominate the ANA church. And there remains the perennial need to educate both ANA believers and the wider world about the distinctions between ANA identity and culture, and identity and culture in Asia itself.

Some years ago I helped lead a worship service in which the cup for Communion was offered two different ways, as either grape juice or as soy milk. In that setting we specially described the soy milk as a way to partake of Jesus' blood in a way associated with ANA culture. (In just the past few years since then, soy milk has pretty much gone mainstream in major supermarkets across America. However, at the time of this particular worship service, soy milk was still the kind of thing you would find in the "Oriental Foods" aisle, if at all.) One of the worshippers at this service was a young biracial woman of Caucasian and Asian ancestry. After the service she remarked to me, "That was the first time I ever connected my Christian faith with the Asian side of me." This was fully half of her life and identity connecting for the first time ever to her faith in Jesus—through a cup of soy milk on the Lord's Table.

I offer the thoughts in this book in hopes that a day will come before very long not only when it will be easy and common to connect Christian faith to ANA identity and culture, but indeed when that connection will be a full and joyful offering from the ANA church to God and to the church worldwide. I pray it will not be very long before one will be able to say "Asian American worship" or "Asian Canadian worship" and many good and joyful things will come to mind. This is not to say that even in the best-case scenario that ANA worship would take on a single shape or flavor. Rather, it is to hope that the search for ANA worship will inspire a sustainable level of passion, creativity, cultural engagement, theological engagement, and purposeful effort. It is to hope that our worship on the Way will become a life-giving journey of discovery.

About Worship and Culture

This is a book about worship and culture. By "worship" I mostly mean what goes on in our churches on Sunday mornings, although this is set in a wider context of beliefs and practices in our families and personal lives, in our wider church communities, and in the overall streams of Christian worship traditions and movements going back to the first century.

By "culture" I mean our shared understandings and shared ways of acting that are related to ethnic identity. We have many other senses of identity too: national, regional, gender, religious, age cohort, institutional (e.g., school and work affiliations), political, class, and so forth, but I am focusing on ethnic identity.

I make a distinction between ethnicity and race. Race is based on physical ancestry and does not change for the individual. (I am only using race in the same sense as the Canadian and United States censuses when they ask for self-identification by race categories.) Ethnicity overlaps with race but is more flexible. One can be of any race and choose to live in an ethnic culture dominated by a different race, such as when a non-Asian chooses to be a member of an Asian Canadian or Asian American church, or, contrariwise, when someone who is racially Asian chooses to identify with the majority culture or a different minority culture, and does not take any particular interest in the ongoing experience and development of his or her ancestral culture. (Even in such cases, however, one's physical self still has its racial identity, so at least that aspect of ethnicity is always present.)

In the United States, "Latino/Hispanic" is an ethnicity, not a race. One can be of any race and be Latino/Hispanic, since it is defined by a shared Spanish-speaking heritage and not by a single place of origin or race. In the same way, I am focusing on Asian North American culture as an ethnic culture, one that greatly overlaps with Asian racial identity in North America but is not identical with it. This book explores how ANA ethnic culture relates to our Sunday morning worship.

Of course, reality is even more complex, since whatever ANA culture is, it is not singular or unchanging. It includes the fifth-generation descendents of Chinese prospectors who came for the 1849 California or 1858 Fraser Canyon gold rushes, all the way to the most recent Karen refugees from Burma arriving this year. It includes those with ancestries throughout the vast landmass that is South, Southeast, and East Asia, with overlap into the Pacific Islands. It includes a range of senses from being "yellow" to being "brown." It includes all the variations from both distant and recent intermarriage (my own ancestry is mostly Chinese from southern China, but there is some possibility that I have a touch of Japanese and possibly even Portuguese blood in me). It includes significant differences between Canada and the United States (described further in Chapter 3). It includes a full range of religious backgrounds, changes, and trajectories. It includes all variations of mixture with both ancestral and majority cultures, as well as other minority cultures. (I myself do not speak Cantonese, but my American-born wife does; meanwhile our children are learning Mandarin.) And it includes rapid, diverse development and change, to include the very emergence of a shared Pan-Asian identity only within the past generation or two. I will refer to "ANA culture" throughout this book but that is shorthand for a very wide and changing range of flavors of ANA experience and identity.

Book Overview

This book was originally conceived as a sourcebook of ANA prayers, graphics, liturgies, and other materials for corporate worship, inspired by Maren C. Tirabassi and Kathy Wonson Eddy's worship sourcebook, *Gifts of Many Cultures: Worship Resources for the Global Community* (Cleveland: Pilgrim Press, 1995). In the course of my research and discussions with the Pacific Asian American Canadian Christian Education (PAACCE) leadership, we discovered that ANA worship is still largely at such an early stage of development that there is simply not yet the range and quantity of materials available for such an extended collection. So this book has become instead more of an exploration and rationale for cultivating an ANA voice and vision in worship. Certainly there are many churches, conference settings, and past and present efforts that have explored and expressed ANA worship. This book offers further encouragement and some helps to continue in such efforts. In the back you will find a sampling of worship materials available for your use but mostly meant to encourage creativity in your own churches.

This book is divided into two sections. Part One is "Explorations of Worship on the Way," discussing matters of culture and worship generally and their applications to ANA culture specifically.

Chapter 1 is an exploration of the relationship between culture and worship. Does culture really matter when it comes to worship? Doesn't Scripture give us all the instructions and details we need to plan worship?

Chapter 2 looks at the cultural trajectory of Scripture from the Old Covenant to the coming of Jesus and the direction of the early church. What is the basic narrative of that trajectory? What are the key passages, and how do they help us understand where we are culturally right now in regards to worship?

Chapter 3 is an attempt to describe and explore Asian North America as a culture, not a place or race. I try to be descriptive and specific enough to be useful without trying to be definitive about what is, after all, still a young culture not fully emerged or expressed.

Chapter 4 is an extended explanation and reflection on worship as transcultural, contextual, countercultural, and cross-cultural (the "Nairobi Statement" categories). How can we avoid getting "stuck" in unhelpful understandings and attitudes toward the role of culture in worship? How can we approach culture with balance, discernment, and skill? How can we bridge the boundaries and barriers between cultures?

Chapter 5 suggests a number of reasons why ANA worship is at an early, perhaps somewhat delayed, state of development. Why are we in this particular state of both need and opportunity? Why is ANA worship a question or problem at all? What particular challenges do we need to address in order to move forward?

Chapter 6 tells stories about a series of my own explorations through several years of worship renewal projects and conferences.

I try to draw out how this journey has hopefully helped me ask better questions and discern promising directions in cultivating ANA worship.

Chapter 7 focuses on the cup of the Lord's Table as a test case for contextualization in worship. Nothing is more culturally specific than food and drink, so a consideration of them helps take us deeply into our ideas and choices about culture and worship. What are our scriptural boundaries and freedoms in worship? Might we have far more freedom than we are used to thinking when it comes to what we set on the Lord's Table?

Chapter 8 goes more deeply into the question of matters of conscience and how to approach such matters as we experiment with different forms in worship. We know everyone has different likes and dislikes in worship forms. But how do we know how far to stretch people? And what might be some helpful strategies for navigating changes in worship forms?

Chapter 9 explores worship among one of the newest ANA immigrant groups: those with Burmese, Karen, Chin, and Kachin ancestries, mostly from Burma (Myanmar) and Thailand, and now with a large number of growing congregations in the American Baptist Churches USA.

Part Two of this book, "Expressions of Worship on the Way," provides a small, suggestive collection of examples of ANA worship. While they are hopefully usable or adaptable for your worship settings, my greater hope is that they can kindle your own creativity and imaginations.

* * * * *

Since ANAs are both a demographic and a cultural minority, the fundamental challenge for ANA worship is specifically a challenge of *biculturality*. The goal is not to somehow recapture ancestral cultures (although those cultures will surely inform parts of the journey). The goal is also not to navigate a smooth assimilation into the majority culture (though that culture belongs to us too). The goal is to be able to bring a full and good offering of ourselves to worship, and the challenge is to do so *when we don't (yet) have a culturally resolved sense of ourselves.* Having received Christian faith largely from majority culture sources (for which we can be thankful as appropriate), we want to now respond with our own voices in worship. But we are still searching for our own voices. We are still asking, "Who am I?" And meanwhile the larger culture continues to ask, "Who are you?" with "forever foreigner" or "honorary white" answers still far too common. This book explores the need for Asian North American worship, a need that exists largely because of the fundamentally bicultural reality and challenge of ANA life.

To be in this early, unsettled stage of cultural identity formation and expression is uncomfortable, but it is not inherently a *problem.* It is not as if we did not study enough for the final exam or didn't work hard enough at the final project, and so find ourselves in this predicament. Rather, I think of this stage as a kind of adolescence. To be a teenager is to be focused on self-discovery and self-formation. (I will explore this metaphor further in the "Crossings" account in Chapter 6.) While one would not want to get stuck in adolescence, it is a stage to be accepted and enjoyed. It is a stage of life especially given to learning, exploring, experimenting, questioning, and discovering. It is also a stage in which important decisions need to be made and important work done, all of which may greatly affect the rest of one's life. I offer this book as a small encouragement and help for those decisions and that work. May the teenager that is ANA worship have a good adolescence. May we be able to look back someday from a stage of well-earned maturity and settled self-understanding, and be grateful for our teenage years.

PART ONE

Explorations of Worship on the Way

CHAPTER 1

Culture Matters

At a church worship service I sat listening to a young Cambodian American woman share about her further steps in her Christian journey. With tears, she related that she had begun to say no to her mom's instructions and requests to participate in various Buddhist rituals and practices: making food offerings to ancestors, lighting incense sticks, wearing a string blessed by a temple monk to ward off evil spirits. Now as a baptized Christian for some years—and with a Christian husband, a child, and a home of her own—she felt she was finally in a position to not go along with such expressions of trust and deference to spirits and beliefs that were rivals to her faith in Jesus.

Not surprisingly, the mother was unhappy about her daughter's choice. Not only did her daughter's nonparticipation threaten the family's well-being, it also threatened the family's very identity. "This is who I am," the mother said. "Don't forget who you are."

Why did the mother assume that living as a Christian meant abandoning Cambodian American culture and identity? Because, in her mind, *there is no such thing as Cambodian American Christianity.* There is no category of being a Christian in a way that well embraces and expresses Cambodian American culture and identity. Whatever happens at church on Sunday is about something other than being Cambodian American, and indeed is effectively a rejection and an abandonment of that ancestral identity.

(Note that the mother specifically linked her identity with the *practice* of Buddhism—with participation in its ritual life at home and temple.)She didn't ask the daughter whether she still believed in reincarnation or which bodhisattva she felt close to. It almost didn't matter what the daughter thought or believed. It was simply a matter of whether she would light the incense, set out the food offerings, and bow for the ancestors. For the mother, performing those rituals was fundamental and essential to Cambodian identity.

But what if going to church on Sunday included worship with movement developed from traditional Cambodian dance? What if somehow there were ways of praying and preaching that specially and redemptively touched the whole experience of the Killing Fields, of the Khmer Rouge, of refugee camps and involuntary migration? What if the Lord's Table were set and served in a recognizably Cambodian way: a low table on a woven mat (approached with shoes off, of course) perhaps with sticky rice for Christ's body and papaya juice for his blood? What if *churches* were notably and happily at the forefront of Cambodian American community work, bilingual language classes, dance and music training, refugee aid, and job placement? What if sermons regularly included Cambodian folk tales, proverbs, historical episodes, and current events? What if greetings and passings of the peace regularly included proper, polite Cambodian titles and forms of address? And what if Christian worship included a full and prominent set of practices honoring and remembering ancestors, perhaps replacing the fear- and anxiety-inducing traditional ancestor rituals with grace-filled, peace-giving, beautifully honoring, and respectful Christian customs?

What if, somehow, it became clear that in order to experience and express Cambodian American culture at its best and fullest, a *Christian church* would be the first place to which you would turn? What if being a follower of Jesus were clearly the *best* way to be Cambodian American? What if the best future of

Cambodian American culture lay in the church—not only in preserving and transmitting ancestral culture, but indeed in redemptively bringing new life, creativity, hope, and beauty out of that culture? What if it were specially because of the church that Cambodian American culture became a beautiful addition to the American multicultural mosaic? Would this mom perceive her daughter's choices differently? Clearly so.

Meanwhile, what is the church missing by not meeting and experiencing Jesus through Cambodian culture? A Christian friend told me of meeting with some young women whose families had recently emigrated from Cambodia. They knew little or nothing about Christianity. He began to tell them about Jesus being the Son of God and being a King. Upon hearing about a king, the girls immediately knelt down—without being prompted or instructed to do so—and bowed their heads to the ground in reverence. (In their culture, such respect for royalty was fully reflexive and internalized.) The state of Cambodian royalty has gone through many twists and turns in recent history but culturally the sense of honor and respect still remains strong. Are there not things that majority-American culture could do well to learn about reverence and adoration—about worship—from such a culture? yes!

A Question for Everyone

Last Sunday at church when somebody up front said, "Let us pray," what did you physically do? You probably closed your eyes, bowed your head, and perhaps folded your hands, all while remaining seated or standing. Why? Not because the Bible told you to pray that way. From Genesis to Revelation, you will not find even one person described as praying with such a posture. (Indeed, in Scripture "closed eyes" are thoroughly negative: a metaphorical reference to death, to callousness to the needy, or to callousness towards God, e.g., Genesis 46:4, Proverbs 28:27,

Isaiah 44:18, Matthew 13:15.) Eyes-closed-head-bowed is a western form of prayer now embedded in our culture. It probably has its roots in early medieval European "commendation" rituals in which a vassal knelt with outstretched hands clasped to pledge fealty to a lord. Today, it is how the American president-elect prays on the inauguration platform when the traditional clergy-led prayer is offered prior to the administration of the oath of office. It is how Queen Elizabeth prayed at the wedding of her grandson, William. It is how people in movies pray. It is part of our culture.

How often at church do you kneel on the floor with your head to the ground? Today we usually associate that posture with Muslim prayer, but you will find plenty of instances of exactly that posture in Scripture (e.g., Genesis 48:12, Nehemiah 8:6, Luke 24:5). How often do you lift your hands up in prayer? Perhaps you are in a Charismatic or Pentecostal worship setting where such a posture is common. Some of our earliest portrayals of prayer in the early church show the "orans" position of standing with hands raised and elbows in. The raising of hands is mentioned several times in the Bible and is even commanded universally in the church (1 Timothy 2:8). Do you literally lift your hands, or do you consider that command a culturally relative reference to be translated into other culturally equivalent gestures (including, perhaps, simply a metaphorical "lifting" of the heart and mind)? Meanwhile, if I told you I "knelt by my bed" you would immediately picture me praying alone, even though nobody in the Bible is described as kneeling by his or her bed. Are not our choices about posture in prayer thoroughly shaped by culture even more so than by Scripture?

Modern western culture places a strong value on practicality. People will say that closing your eyes helps reduce distraction. That may often be true (especially for grade-school children in Sunday school), but is that then forever the primary reason for choosing a default prayer posture? Other Christian traditions use icons and other visual objects for prayer, which provide focus and thus reduce distraction in a different way. But icons take more work and are thus less practical than simply closing one's eyes. Bowing to the ground, face to the floor, reduces a lot of distractions too but perhaps feels like a distraction to others. It also takes up more room than just sitting or standing. It's not as practical. A student of mine tells of being at a gas station one day, with a line growing and no one being helped. Looking more closely at the booth he discovered the attendant on the floor, kneeling with his head to the ground. What are the odds that the attendant was an American Christian saying the Lord's Prayer in such time and manner?

We actually have the freedom to use *any* of these postures and practices, or any others, but we should be honest about our (cultural) reasons for what we choose to do. Without that honesty we are likely to consider our practices "right" or "best" in ways that are really not justified, and look down judgmentally on those with different practices from ours. When a child asks, "Why do we close our eyes when we pray?" we can say, "That's how you pray" (and what happens when that child grows up and realizes the Bible never says to close your eyes to pray?). Or we can say, "It's one way to pray; it helps us to be less distracted. Sometimes we can try other ways people pray too." Do you see the difference? Without that honesty about the culturally relative reasons for our practices, we will not understand our practices for what they are, and we will not be open to other practices that may be good and helpful, especially practices that involve cultural stretching or creativity.

Does culture really matter? Can't we all just worship the Christian way (whatever that is)? Aren't matters of culture divisive? Doesn't an emphasis on culture risk the worshipping of culture rather than Christ? And if culture does matter, isn't it an issue mostly for worshippers from immigrant, minority groups and not more established churches?

Questions of culture may be obvious and pressing for cultural minority groups but such questions actually surround each and every worship setting. Majority-culture churches, every bit as much as immigrant churches, are shaped by cultural matters of language, music, time, schedule, posture, gesture, movement, deportment, gender, generation, architecture, decoration, furniture, technology, dress, and leadership. Why does your church's music use a twelve-tone equal temperament scale based on an A = 440 Hz tuning? Why do church buildings in your neighborhood have crosses as architectural features? Why does the person up front speaking in your worship service generally stand up while everyone else sits down? These are all matters of culture.

And these are all matters that Scripture largely leaves up to us. There is not one complete worship service even *described* in any detail in the New Testament, let alone *prescribed*. You could not plan a worship service using only details found in Scripture because there are not remotely enough details there. You could not recreate with certainty even just for historical interest what happened on any given Sunday in Jerusalem, Corinth, or Rome. We can guess and infer from what we know of the history and peoples of those times and places, especially the varieties of Jewish synagogue and temple worship in which Christian worship has its roots. We can read between the lines of what we do have in Scripture: some general references to gathering, teaching, singing, praising, collecting freewill offerings, and such; some snippets of liturgical creeds, hymns, prayers, and formulas ("Amen," "Alleluia"); some negative examples (the rich in Corinth not waiting to eat together with the poor); and some partial descriptions of particular rituals like Baptism and the Lord's Table. But we do not have even one example of a complete worship order. And even if we did—say, a copy of Priscilla's notes for a service in Ephesus—we would not know how representative it was. Worship must have varied from place to place and over time, probably greatly, and often in unpredictable ways. Scripture not only does not command the details of worship; it largely doesn't provide what we might like to know even for curiosity's sake.

What if all I knew about worship at your church were some passing references you made in a few blog entries: "I really liked today's worship leader, especially what she shared about that song about forgiveness." "Today Deacon Nguyen preached because the pastor was out of town." "The new couple got baptized today, both of them." "We remembered you in the prayers of the people." "After church there were three different kinds of adobo at the potluck." From such mentions, how much could I recreate of what actually happened at your church? Even if we both spoke the same language, shared the same ancestry, were born into the same generation, and were raised in the same city, I still could only guess very generally. Yet that is the nature of most of what we know from the New Testament about the details of worship in the early church.

Even the practice of weekly Sunday worship is not actually mentioned (let alone commanded) in Scripture. All we have are three faint hints. We have the account of Paul's longwinded talk at Troas on "the first day of the week" (Acts 20:7), but this is precisely a special gathering for a visiting preacher. Paul gives instructions to set aside donations for the Jerusalem support fund "on the first day of every week" (1 Corinthians 16:2), but the context says nothing directly about corporate worship. And John describes his initial revelation occurring on the "Lord's day" (Revelation 1:10), but that is the only New Testament use of that phrase and we cannot know for certain what John meant (although later in church history it came to mean Sunday as the day of worship). Christian worship did migrate quite early on from the Jewish Sabbath (the seventh day) to Sunday (the first day) but we don't know how, when, where, or why this happened (although we can guess that it was because every Sunday became a "little Easter," celebrating Jesus' resurrection). So every church with weekly Sunday morning worship is not "worshipping the way the Bible says" but rather is exercising its freedom to order and shape worship using various inherited cultural forms.

(The bottom line is this: we not only have the freedom to use culture to help shape worship, we really don't have any choice but to do so.) Scripture not only gives us the freedom to shape and order our worship life, it *requires* that we exercise that freedom. What Scripture is mostly concerned with is the *object* of our worship: God as revealed in Jesus Christ. Scripture does give us a full range of *functions* in worship: praise, petition, proclamation, thanksgiving, confession, lament, teaching, exhortation, offering, a water ritual of initiation, and a table ritual of remembrance and nourishment. But all the *forms* of worship are largely left to us—which is to say the forms and details are largely and inherently matters of culture.

Freedoms from Forms

Forms in worship are both good and unavoidable. Why should that surprise us? Every artist can only be creative within the boundaries of a medium, technique, and subject matter. Every athlete can only compete if there are rules and measurements. And every church and worship tradition can only create and sustain a worship life by making a good use of forms. (Real freedom in worship only comes from using forms well. Freedoms come from forms, not from avoiding or discarding them.)

In public life we happily embrace and celebrate endless rituals and forms. Think of the Olympic Games: the procession of national teams, the lighting of the Olympic Flame, and the medal ceremonies broadcast to top ratings worldwide. Think of Changing the Guard by ceremonial sentries whether at Buckingham palace or anywhere else, watched by endless crowds. Think of standing for national anthems such as "O Canada" and "The Star-Spangled Banner" and royal anthems such as "God Save the Queen." Think of our many holiday traditions including ethnic minority festivals such as Lunar New Year. And then there are our rituals and forms in private life and semi-public life, such as all our customs around birthdays, weddings, funerals, graduations, and so on. While creativity and change can be good, it is actually the continuity of forms that carries the deepest level of meaning. We say the same marriage vows that have been said for centuries: "to have and to hold from this day forward, for better for worse, for richer for poorer, in sickness and in health, to love and to cherish." It is precisely the larger tradition that gives meaning to our individual lives and to each succeeding generation. And it is only within a framework of tradition that our creativity can be freed: the dancing bridal procession, the clever wedding cake, the memorably apt toast. Freedoms are built on a foundation of good forms.

That we are usually not very self-aware about our worship forms is not surprising. If we are part of a majority culture and our worship setting draws mostly from that culture, then we get used to our particular cultural "flavor" of worship being "normal." For instance, coming from an industrialized, technological culture, we are entirely used to having technology permeate our worship settings. Artificial lights, electronically amplified sound, projected images, mechanical heating and cooling, pasteurized grape juice for Communion, indoor plumbing, printed books, clocks, parking lots, and of course the inevitable unsilenced cell phone ringtone—we don't think twice about such technological aspects of our worship settings. We also don't find it unusual if these same things are found in school, work, and entertainment settings outside church (e.g., the same pasteurized grape juice for school lunch). It just seems normal to us, a given for how such things are done. Nothing about such aspects of our culture strikes us as *unchristian* because we live in a majority-Christian culture and these elements happen to be everyday parts of that culture.

So, to start (and hopefully end, or at least intend to) "on time"—that is, at a repeating, preannounced, round increment of daily clock time—is embedded into our Sunday worship, because it's part of our culture. Might other cultures pay less attention to clocks, or no attention at all? It would hardly do to quote 1 Corinthians 14:40 and say, no, everything must be done "decently and in order" and therefore we must start and end "on time." Cultures differ widely in what they consider decent and orderly. Back when public phone booths were the norm, the Japanese had little colored signal lights on theirs that a caller could switch on to indicate to anyone waiting for the phone how much longer they were likely to have to wait. How decent! In German cities there are small metal plates on the ground level outside of commercial and public buildings detailing the placement and depth of underground pipes emerging from the building. How orderly! Both cultures have a numerically precise sense of decency and orderliness. In contrast, a cousin of mine in Hawaii tells me that a luau on the beach initiated by locals might well start anytime from late morning to late afternoon—really, there isn't a sense of "starting" because people just come when they come and at some point everyone will have been there. In such a culture, it would be indecent to constrain one's 'ohana "family, community" to an artificial, mechanical structure of arriving and departing. And these are all matters of culture.

To cite another example of how our forms are shaped by culture: we generally think nothing of mixed-gender seating in church. But any anthropologist or sociologist can tell you that such casualness about mixed company is hardly universal in history or in contemporary cultures. When my wife and I had an opportunity to do some study in Jerusalem and went one day to pray at the Western Wall, we could not pray together. The Wall is treated as an Orthodox synagogue, with men and women praying in separate designated areas. If I had been raised in such a culture and later came to worship at pretty much any North American Christian church, would I not have sensitivities about the mixed seating? Would anyone care to hear me point out that mixed seating introduces an element of sexual distraction and a greater opportunity for improper thoughts? Would anyone take me seriously if I proposed an option of segregated seating for those who might prefer it? (I realize gender segregation has historically been tied very closely to gender hierarchy in worship settings. I am not trying to downplay that important issue, but it is not my point here.) Can you think of any church you've ever visited that did not have mixed seating? Why is that? Is this not a cultural choice we have simply accepted as a given?

I could go on with virtually every aspect of our Sunday worship, tracing the forms of our actual practices back to this or that cultural development rather than to Scriptural prescriptions. It is only as we understand the cultural reasons for our forms that we can better understand that these forms are not set in stone, that they were the products of past changes and can become the subjects of future changes. We can better understand that these forms may or may not be best for our particular worship settings or traditions, that there may be some cultural mismatches that need to be addressed. We can also understand that we neither have nor need rationally defensible, documented reasons for every form, because sometimes perfectly usable forms arise from happenstance (Christmas as December 25), long-forgotten circumstances (weekly Sunday worship), or even misunderstanding ("Jehovah" from a misreading of the Hebrew *kethiv/qere* for YHWH). We cannot make good use of our freedoms regarding forms in worship until we understand the nature of such forms and we accept such freedoms.

In Search of Forms

Making good use of forms is a particular challenge for much of Protestant worship, especially in the free worship traditions that dominate the ANA church. In such traditions we have more freedom than anyone to shape and lead our worship—we can reinvent it every Sunday if we wish. But meanwhile we make use of perhaps the fewest resources for shaping and leading our worship, at least besides considerable resources for band-led congregational singing. We do not have an inherited liturgical tradition to provide a full framework and pattern for our worship. We do not have a tradition of wide and deep scholarly reflection on matters of worship history and theology, and thus we often don't know what our options are, how to evaluate them, or even how to talk about them. We do not even have a settled sense of the relative uses of ritual, personality, and creativity.

Mostly what we have and use is a pragmatic sensibility of "What works?" alongside a mostly unreflective use of inherited patterns and habits. With all our freedom, how many of our worship services are pretty much the same pattern inherited from North American frontier and then urban revivalism: gathering music, prayers and announcements, a sermon, perhaps the Lord's Table, then response music? For all our freedom, the worship in so many of our churches ends up looking remarkably similar. As the saying goes, "When people are free to do as they please, they usually imitate each other."

In some circles, the immediate work and leading of the Holy Spirit is presumed to require an open discarding of anything previously planned, scheduled, or required, including any dependence on an inherited ritual tradition. It's as if orders of worship are at best a necessary evil, an administrative chore to be discarded as quickly as possible so that the Spirit can "really move." It seems to me that such thinking is precisely just another restriction on ways the Holy Spirit is allowed to work. The Spirit's freedom surely includes the freedom to use both planned and spontaneous moments, to use an ancient liturgy or an extemporaneous prayer, and to use an official service book or a lightly structured ad hoc gathering. The freedom of the Spirit is not a freedom from form (if that were even possible), but a freedom to use all manner of forms, including the occasional unplanned form.

It would be as if a teacher were presumed to only be "really teaching" when going off the lesson plan. A good teacher will certainly go off the lesson plan from time to time when the classroom flow calls for it, but will mostly stay on plan and will do most of the teaching as planned. Indeed, it is only by staying on-plan that any off-plan moments might be possible. Of course, even "staying on plan" can look very different for different teachers who are equally effective. And there may be cases when a poor plan (perhaps dictated by an ineffective administration, or designed for an earlier generation of students) is worth discarding. But the problem there is a poor plan. Something ad hoc might be better than something poorly planned, yet a steady dependence on the ad hoc is a dance with chaos, and inevitably leads to its own forms, most likely not very good forms at that.

(The only alternative to a good use of forms is a bad use of forms.) The greatest hazard is for churches to think that freedom from required or necessary forms is a freedom from all forms. Too often such churches end up with a mishmash of forms that are unrecognized as such and are not well-created or well-used. Such supposed freedom too often results in chatty, strained calls to worship ("Good morning! ['Good morning'] Oh come on, you can do better than that!... "), deadweight formulas ("May God add a special blessing to anyone who cannot give"), and paltry expressions of quasi-authenticity ("Lord, I just...I...I just want to pray for..."). These are all forms, and such formulas are frequently used even more rigidly than formal liturgies. Even when forms may be enduringly good and usable (say, regularly singing Thomas Ken's 1674 lyric, "Praise God from whom all blessings flow..." to the 1551 Genevan Psalter hymn tune now known as "OLD 100th"), we need an informed, balanced sensibility about why to use such an ingrained but not required form, why we may or may not change it, and how to even talk about such decisions.

Since, by God's evident design, Scripture largely does not dictate those forms, we must use our own cultural resources in a wise, loving, skillful, and creative way. This will involve not blindly embracing majority-culture forms as simply "the way we do it" or, worse, as "the Christian way." And, for those of us in minority-culture churches, it will involve exploring our cultures for new forms that can convey well the offering of our worship.

Responsibility and Opportunity

It would certainly be easier if Scripture gave us a cookbook for Sunday services, with the details and actions all directed and scripted out. We wouldn't have to make any decisions! We would know exactly how we are to dress and the exact words of each prayer. We would not have to spend one second trying to decide where to put the announcements or whether candles are appropriate. We would know exactly how to start and end each service. It sure would save time and effort!

Such a cookbook for worship would also make it easy to know if we were doing things the *right way*. This felt need for validation is rarely discussed, but I believe it runs very deep and shapes a great deal of what happens on Sundays. We want to know that worship was designed and led properly, that God was addressed correctly in our prayers, and that we didn't leave out anything essential in preparing and serving the Lord's Table. We want to know that we did the right things in worship so we can know that worship really happened.

But Scripture is more a portrait than a cookbook, more a story than a how-to guide. As in so much of the faith journey, God really does treat us like adults, asking us to be responsible to make choices and then to live with those choices. As with each of our individual lives, God gives us open opportunities to order and shape our shared worship lives. God invites us to respond to that portrait and to enter into that story in ways that emerge from the creativity and skills given to us. God seems to care far more about our growth in love and wisdom (which are what good worship planning always

15

require) than about particular forms and details. We see in creation that God loves variety, and we see this as well in our creative work of worship. Surely this love of variety is in part to simply express, in the widest possible variety of cultures and settings, God's infinite beauty and character. All the cultures in history all over the world could not together fully express the breadth and depth of God's self-offering to us. Yet, being created in God's image, we are made to be creators too, so we creatively go about worship in all of our different cultures and settings.

Thus we need all different kinds of worship settings, from the most ancient Greek Orthodox liturgy to the most experimental postmodern, hip-hop, techno-worship (and whatever will come after that); from the jewel that is black Baptist worship to the most gloriously "plain" Amish service; from worship at a major cathedral to Sundays at a small, trilingual French-English-Chinese Québécois church taking tentative steps in mixing host and ancestral cultures; and everything in between. This need for variety is all the more pressing since culture is never fixed or singular, especially in the urban, cosmopolitan centers of North America where the vast majority of Asian North Americans live. We need all different kinds of churches for all different kinds of cultures and communities. As cultures mix and change we need new forms of worship in which God can be met. And God has given us the freedom to receive all these present and future cultures as good gifts for worship.

Cultural Validation

But across the range of such variety, where do we turn to for validation in our worship choices? How do we know what our norms and boundaries are? How do we gauge whether we are doing a good job with our worship forms?

Different worship traditions turn to different sources for their main sense of validation in worship. Liturgical traditions would seem to have it the easiest: they have official service books so it's pretty straightforward to tell if the liturgy was followed (although most such service books involve far more options, opportunities to extemporize, and overall possibilities for creativity than many non-liturgical worshippers might imagine). Charismatic and Pentecostal traditions look more to manifestations of the immediate work of the Holy Spirit, especially as expressed in the physical and emotional experiences of the worshippers—were people "touched" by the Spirit in some visible way? Did the leaders exhibit an "anointing" that seemed to go beyond human effort and ability? Traditions that emphasize expository preaching have a sensibility about whether Scripture was handled properly and taught with the necessary authority and correct doctrine. Worship in the American mainline churches and the United Church of Canada has generally shed much of its denominational worship distinctives and tends to emphasize organizational and affiliational identity. Emergent worship settings have their own aesthetics and hallmarks about whether the worship discourse was sufficiently vulnerable and open-ended, whether there was an appropriate "edginess," and whether the worship space was interactive and evocative without being directive.

And that can all be for the good. One of the best reasons to have and sustain a wide variety of worship traditions is that we need each other to preserve, transmit, and develop our various particular approaches, our particular slices of the worship spectrum. But within each tradition, the different sources of validation can be used and misused, each with its own particular strengths and weaknesses.

In this book I want to emphasize one particular area of validation that applies to every flavor of worship: *are we expressing, engaging, and developing the cultures of our worshippers well*? As people come to church, do they sense that Jesus is God come in the flesh *for their people*; that God hears and delights in their particular cultural "voice"; that the gospel is truly Good News for every sorrow and joy in their people's story; that they have uniquely valuable gifts of heritage, history, and experience that very much need to be shared as Good News for others? As far as I can tell, there are scant places in the ANA church where one could readily and regularly answer yes to such questions. What is worse, there are few places where such needs are even felt and recognized.

Designing and planning worship is hard enough in majority-culture settings with an inheritance of fully formed traditions, landmark church buildings, and whole denominational departments producing worship materials. It is even harder in minority-culture settings with an inheritance of conflation (western = Christian), neglect, additional big issues (what to do with ancestor worship?), bicultural tension, and theological underdevelopment (what is the Good News for "model minority" high achievers?). Here at least the Canadian church has the advantage of a well-established consensus around multiculturalism, that extends to the highest governmental levels (an officially bilingual nation, a full recognition of the fundamental place of First Nations peoples, a series of federal laws around multiculturalism and official vocabulary and policies about "visible minorities"). But across the continent the door for recognizable, sustainable developments in ANA worship remains essentially wide open. We not only have the special responsibilities and opportunities of every minority-culture worship setting, we also have the further responsibilities and opportunities of being cultural pioneers in worship.

I started off this chapter with a Cambodian American example of the need for ANA forms of worship. If such forms are so needed, why haven't they been forthcoming? Would they really be worth the effort? What more can we find in Scripture to help with such work? What are the issues that need to be faced and what are helpful ways to talk about them? And could this really happen—could we really create and use such forms and find ourselves (and others) thankful that we did so? That is what the rest of this book will explore.

CHAPTER 2

Words from the Word

In Chapter 1 I made the point at length that the Bible tells us very little about the details of worship forms. However, some texts are essential for our exploration of worship and culture. In this chapter we'll take a look at some of those Scriptures. First, we'll look at two commandments that overarch our entire consideration of worship. Then we'll look at the new cultural trajectory in God's plan that began with the coming of Jesus.

All You Need to Know in Two Commandments

When it comes to matters of worship and culture, we would do well to start with Jesus' reply to the scribes (who were experts in the Jewish law) about what is the most important commandment:

> Jesus answered, "The first is, 'Hear, O Israel: the Lord our God, the Lord is one; you shall love the Lord your God with all your heart, and with all your soul, and with all your mind, and with all your strength.' The second is this, 'You shall love your neighbor as yourself.' There is no other commandment greater than these." (Mark 12:29-31)

Monotheism requires exclusive loyalty. If there were several gods or many gods, we would need to parcel out our devotion: our family life to one god, our finances to another, our work life

19

to another, and so forth. But if there is one and only one God, then that God is the proper object of the whole of our devotion, our whole heart, soul, mind, and strength. (Like "flesh and blood" [Matthew 16:17] for "human," this fourfold description in Mark's version and the slightly different parallel versions in Matthew and Luke are most likely a way of saying, "with all you are"—a synecdoche, naming some parts to express the whole.) I call this first commandment the _rule of self-offering_. We are called to offer all we are to God, the whole of our selves—the visible and the invisible, all of our being and effort.

(Does this self-offering include who we are in our racial, cultural, and ethnic identities? What if for some reason I had to set aside every part of me that is connected to my ANA ancestry, upbringing, self-identification, and ongoing life? That would include my family name, my choice of spouse (a fellow Chinese American whom I married happily almost twenty-five years ago), much of how I relate to my parents and extended family, how I approach my work and responsibilities, how I interact with those "above" and "below" me in group situations, what I choose to eat about half the time, many of the values I try to teach my children, the writing of this book, many of my own internal questions and issues about identity, the color of my hair and eyes, and on and on. Could I set aside all that and still make a good and full self-offering to God? Clearly not. If I am to love God with all I am, that will have to include who I am in my ANA identity and culture.)

An African American pastor who is involved in racial reconciliation work once told me about a not uncommon encounter he had with another leader of a different race than his. This leader said to him, "I want you to know that when I look at you I _don't see a black man._" Such a thought was surely well intentioned, desiring to express that race was not a barrier to relating to each other across America's most intractable racial divide. Nevertheless, the African American pastor's response was to take off his own glasses, lean way in, and say, "Here, let me help you." We are who we are, as God has made us, including everything about our physical ancestry, bodies, cultural heritages, and presence. To love God with all we are is to make a full and good self-offering of all we are.

Indeed, the African American church, perhaps especially in its black Baptist expressions, is arguably the preeminent example of an American racial minority culture that has found its own voice in worship in a fully powerful and redemptive way. Indeed, I regularly cite black Baptist worship as the crown jewel of American worship, where a people's history, struggles, joys, and life come together in a fully present, fully expressed, fully embodied, fully energized, fully Christian way. The traditions of gathering and being wholly present, the gospel music, the praying and preaching, the call-and-response between the worship leaders and congregation, the full vocabulary of gesture and movement—this is a people who have found their own voice in worship, even in the face of their often crushing needs for more leadership development and Christian formation. Of all the forms of worship developed in America—frontier revivalism (and its modern incarnations such as the seeker-sensitive movement), the voluntary church, the use of unfermented grape juice for communion, worship via broadcast media, and aspects of the emergent worship movement—one would be hard pressed to name a stronger and more life-giving example of a people's full and good self-offering in worship than black Baptist worship.

The good self-offering that is black Baptist worship has indeed gone on to become a striking gift to the wider world. In content and delivery, what was Martin Luther King Jr.'s "I Have a Dream" speech on the steps of the Lincoln Memorial on August 28, 1963, but a black Baptist sermon? This sermon is now considered among the greatest and most important speeches in American history, on the level of Lincoln's Gettysburg Address and Second Inaugural Address carved into the walls of that very Memorial. Meanwhile, buses full of European tourists line up every Sunday outside some of the landmark black Baptist churches in New York City, hoping to glimpse this storied form of worship. The influence of black gospel music on western popular culture has been incalculable. In my hometown of Oakland, one rarely hears an invocation or other prayer at a civic or public gathering—unless a prominent member of the city's black clergy offers it. One would rarely hear church music at such a gathering were it not sung by our (fabulous!) Interfaith Gospel Choir. Such is the power of a full and good self-offering in worship.

But Jesus did not stop with the rule of self-offering. He went on to pronounce the second greatest commandment: "Love your neighbor as yourself." I call this the *rule of self-sacrifice*. If my neighbor (that is, anyone in my life) has a background and values similar to mine, this love may not be especially hard. If we vote the same, have the same tastes in music, feel the same way about things happening in our neighborhood, drive comparable cars, have compatible approaches to parenting, share overlapping ancestries and cultures, and appreciate the same kinds of food, it will not feel like a great sacrifice to care for each other.

But Jesus did not say, "Love your like-minded, likeable neighbor as yourself." He just said "your neighbor," which includes everyone you know—including those who vote exactly opposite from the way you do, listen to music you find irritating and contemptible, volunteer for causes you consider wrongheaded and immoral, drive cars you would not care to be seen driving even if someone offered to give them to you for free, and so on. You are to love them in the same way you love yourself. You are to value them and care about their well-being as much as you do for yourself.

What Self-Sacrifice Is *Not*

Note that even here Jesus allows and expects you to love yourself. Before you can make a sacrifice of yourself, you have to embrace yourself—or else what do you have to sacrifice? I have some friends who recently returned from several years of life and ministry in Central America. I was thanking one of them for her excellent worship music leadership at our church. "It's so nice to lead in English again!" she whispered. Bless her for all the Spanish-language worship leading she had been doing. That was sacrificial precisely because Spanish was not her mother tongue. But even while still in Central America no one would have expected her to abhor English. When Paul wrote, "I have become all things to all people, so that I might by all means save some" (1 Corinthians 9:22), he was not rejecting his own culture and identity, but rather speaking of his freedom to be adaptable. He had the best freedom of all, the freedom to know, love, value, and honor himself and his heritage fully while being able to freely set himself aside as needed to love others.

Since ANA culture is still young and in formation, there is a sense in which we do not yet have a "mother tongue" in which to become fluent. We also often exhibit a Confucian readiness to be deferential and accommodating to other cultures. As a result, I think we sometimes risk being too ready to resist or deny our God-created identity. A humble willingness to self-sacrifice may in practice be an exercise in self-rejection. This is one of the reasons I think there certainly is room and need for ANA-focused churches. I worry that jumping to multicultural stages of church life might skip needed stages of our own ANA cultural and identity development. The rule of self-offering does come first, before the rule of self-sacrifice, which only makes sense. There needs to be a self that can be embraced and offered before that self can also be sacrificed.

We need to avoid a semblance of self-sacrifice that is actually an unhelpful urge to assimilate, or worse, an actual self-hatred. I myself came of age in California in the assimilationist currents of the 1970s, where the idea was to mostly blend in, not highlight your minority ancestry, and speak only English. I remember thinking of first-generation immigrant Chinese as "them," not "us." I don't think I looked down on immigrants in terms of value (after all, they could speak the endlessly magical, endlessly mysterious ancestral tongue), but I definitely saw myself as happily "ahead" of them in the journey of assimilation.

I now look back and consider it my loss that I did not make more of an effort to learn more from such immigrants, because I would have discovered many things about myself. As an adult, when I spent a season on staff at a mostly white church, I realized much more just how Chinese I really am. (I remember, for instance, being regularly taken aback by how readily some people in the church told me—a young pastoral intern—quite revealing details of their lives. I had not realized how different the interpersonal boundaries were in Asian vs. Caucasian cultures.) Later in life I also came to meet Asian American friends who had grown up with a biculturality that was often the worst of both worlds, a painfully confusing series of mixed messages, cultural embarrassments, and longings to be anything but themselves. They, especially, and even I (who mostly grew up thinking of being bicultural as having the best of both worlds) probably had work to do before being ready to fully engage in self-sacrifice. Self-understanding and self-acceptance come before self-sacrifice.

Self-Offering and Self-Sacrifice in Worship

How do these two commandments apply to worship? The rule of self-offering tells us it is vital to find and use our own voices and visions in worship—voices and visions that authentically express our identities, cultures, and life experiences; voices and visions that bring to God as fully as possible our particular joys, sorrows, hopes, struggles, disappointments, stories, and longings. This law of self-offering says that the gifts we bring to worship should be our selves as fully as possible, the gift of the people and lives God made in making us. And this surely includes all the ways being ANA in ancestry and culture contribute to who we are, whether obvious ways (like our outward appearance) or more subtle ways (such as a tendency to be more reserved and deferential than the majority culture). (Only when we can make a full self-offering in worship can we love God in worship with all we are.)

Meanwhile, the rule of self-sacrifice tells us it is vital to honor and nurture the voices and visions of others in worship, including all those who come from cultural backgrounds quite different from yours or mine. This includes those who are First Nations peoples; descendents of African slaves, of Mayflower passengers, and of Charlottetown Conference participants; recent immigrants from Mexico and Latin and South America; refugees from Ethiopia; and everyone else who lives in the same towns and cities where we live. People of every background and culture are called to make their own self-offering just as we are. So we are responsible to love them by helping them make as full and good a self-offering in worship as possible.

Moreover, the rule of self-sacrifice applies to each of us individually. I am to love my neighbor as myself whether that neighbor is a fellow ANA three generations removed from me, or a fellow ANA whose ancestors and mine despised and killed each other, or someone old enough to be my grandparent or young enough to be my child, or someone of the opposite gender, or someone who reminds me of aspects of my culture I do not like, or someone I do not like for simple reasons of personality. I am to love that neighbor by valuing that neighbor's worship life and doing what I can to help that neighbor make as full and good a self-offering in worship as possible.

Applying the Rules to Worship Styles

Let's think about how these rules of self-offering and self-sacrifice apply to one of the most regularly challenging aspects of worship: what styles of music to use on Sunday morning.

By the rule of self-offering it follows that music in the worship service should be of a style that speaks as directly and fully as possible to and from the hearts of a particular gathering of worshippers. The music should emerge deeply and truly from their identity and life experiences; it should fit their personality and cultural manners; it should be connected to their memories, aspirations, and sense of self; it should touch their particular sorrows and express their particular joys. It should be fully *their* music. (There is a tension here, of course, between all of this as it applies to a given individual and to a group. One measure of a group's maturity is the degree to which individual and group identities actually nurture each other.)

By the rule of self-sacrifice it follows that if I am responsible for Sunday music, the first question I should ask is not "What do *I* like?" but rather, "What will best help *others* to make their best self-offering?" In an age of seemingly ubiquitous earbuds, MP3 downloads, and satellite car radios, the prevailing assumption when it comes to music is that *everyone has a right to listen to the music he or she likes*. On one hand, the music I like is connected to my good and full self-offering—this is the music that best expresses my voice and most directly conveys my thoughts and feelings from the language of my heart. On the other hand, I am called to die to myself (Matthew 10:39).

To be sure, Jesus promises me I will "find my life" in the process of losing it, which will include finding a music I can truly call my own. But finding my life comes not by selfishly defending my music as something I need and must have (if so, it has become an idol for me), but rather precisely by getting myself out of the way as much as possible. Things become mine not by grasping but by letting go. And in the process, perhaps I will find that getting myself out of the way opens me to "find myself" in a much wider range of music than I ever imagined.

This rule of self-sacrifice can only be worked out relationally. What two contending musical factions in a church will do when each resolves to put the other first is not something that can be worked out logically, for it is a logical paradox. It can only be worked out in real, living relationships in which the process of working it out will be as important as the outcome.

The process may involve one side deferring to the other for a season for the sake of outreach. It may involve the younger deferring to the older to honor them and to make the most of their fewer remaining years, or the older deferring to the younger to give them better prospects for their more numerous remaining years. It may involve attending to other weaknesses in the fabric of a church community so that its musical life need not be so much of its "glue." It may involve discovering, adapting, or inventing new styles of music. It may involve integrating different styles in a single service or segregating them into separate services. It may involve a sustained program of music education and exposure to visiting musicians.

Whatever it may involve, this inherently relational process will always start by asking "How can I love my neighbor?" and then persevering through the hard relational and ministry work that follows. And it is a journey in which ANA worshippers live with the tension of being between ancestral culture, the majority culture, nearby minority cultures, and ANA culture itself. Like two oars in a rowboat, the rules of self-offering and self-sacrifice together can help us navigate through these tensions.

With the rule of self-offering and the rule of self-sacrifice in mind, we are now ready to take a look at the cultural trajectory of Scripture.

From Centripetal to Centrifugal

For many centuries, God's central plan for salvation was focused on one culture, the Jewish culture, built around the law as given to Moses at Mt. Sinai. From the beginning, Jews were called to be a light to the nations and the means of salvation for all. But from the time of Moses until the time of Jesus, becoming a believer required becoming *culturally Jewish*. Anyone from any culture could become a believer in Yahweh, but this involved adopting the whole law of Moses, including the dietary laws, the sacrifices, circumcision, everything. For a Gentile to become a believer in the God of Israel required living culturally with the people of Israel. A good example is Ruth, a Moabite by ancestry, who chose to live as a Jew with her Jewish mother-in-law, Naomi. "Where you go, I will go; Where you lodge, I will lodge; your people shall be my people, and your God my God" (Ruth 1:16). Culturally, this is motion to the center, or *centripetal* motion.

Jesus took this centripetal cultural exclusivity and turned it around to a *centrifugal* direction, motion outward from the center and towards all directions. In his early ministry, Jesus himself both kept the law and pointed toward its passing—or, more accurately, its fulfillment. One of the most striking claims he made to his divinity was claiming to be the "Lord of the Sabbath" (Luke 6:5). He thus asserted his full authority over the interpretation, enforcement, and revision of one of the Ten Commandments, this one rooted in the very creation order, and a pillar of Jewish life and identity. To relax the laws and traditions around Sabbath keeping was in part to reverse the culturally centripetal direction of God's salvation plan. Jesus claimed personal authority to institute such a change. Likewise, in his further debates over the role of the Mosaic law, he set in motion the removal of kosher dietary restrictions, so that it could actually be said in retrospect, "Thus he declared all foods clean" (Mark 7:19). In the centripetal phase, all believers had to shop at kosher grocery stores. With the coming of Jesus and the start of the centrifugal phase, all believers could shop wherever they wished (including the kosher grocery store).

In his conversation with a Samaritan woman, Jesus unmoored true worship from its one divinely situated location in Jerusalem and declared it could soon take place anywhere (say, beside a well in Samaria!) as long as it was "in spirit and truth" (John 4:23-24). Before his ascension, Jesus' Great Commission to his followers was to make disciples of "all nations" to the "ends of the earth" (Matthew 28:19-20, Acts 1:8). This of course would include people of all different cultures. But would this be on the pattern of the Mosaic law, with new believers from those diverse cultures adopting the Jewish way of life and worship? Or might things take a quite different turn?

The first half of the book of Acts gives the dramatic answer to that question. In Acts 2, Jesus' promised gift of the Holy Spirit arrived on the birthday of the church and brought a cultural birthday gift: the disciples were given the ability to speak the languages of all the different parts of the Roman Empire from which the gathered Jewish pilgrims hailed. Now, what if the miracle had instead been that all these diaspora Jews were given the gift of complete fluency in Hebrew? (That is to say, what if the *centripetal* trajectory toward a single cultural "center" had simply continued?) The Holy Spirit could have surely arranged such a miracle just as easily. But of course, that is not what happened; rather, "each one heard them speaking in the native language of each" (Acts 2:6). The chaos of Babel became the chorus of the church—though a chorus both then and still now in need of much rehearsal, training, and encouragement. The new outward, *centrifugal* trajectory was not a cultural monotone but a diverse unity of cultures and languages.

Guess Who's Coming to Dinner?

In Acts, the particular story that gets the most ink begins in chapter 10 with Peter's encounter with Cornelius. You remember the story: one day around lunchtime Peter was praying and getting sleepy. (I'm glad I'm not the only one that happens to, especially after eating!) He fell into a trance and received a vision from God of all kinds of animals, clean (kosher) and unclean (non-kosher). "Kill and eat," said the voice. "Surely not, Lord!" Peter replied. After some back and forth, the voice from heaven said, "Do not call anything impure that God has made clean" (Acts 10:13-15, NIV). What exactly had God made clean?

A Gentile Roman army officer named Cornelius had been devoutly seeking and serving God as best he knew how, doing good works for the poor and also praying. Peter's assignment was to go to the house of Cornelius and tell him the Good News of Jesus. Peter was to do something he had possibly never done before in his life: step foot in the home of Gentiles and accept their hospitality—including partaking of any non-kosher meal served. Peter was to treat that Gentile home as a worthy and "clean" setting in which Jesus (a Jewish Savior of what was then still an overwhelmingly Jewish movement) could be proclaimed and followed.

God could have just as easily—indeed, more easily—asked Cornelius to go to Peter's house and adapt to kosher ways before he could hear the Good News. But no, it was Peter who had to now recognize that other cultures were worthy settings in which God could be met, served, and worshipped—that *Gentile cultures are acceptable,* that God had made them *clean.* (This was not to say that Gentile culture or any culture did not have elements that needed to be redeemed or even rejected. I will discuss this further in Chapter 4.)

It might be worth noting that Cornelius's acceptable culture notwithstanding, he still needed Jesus, this very Jewish *Yeshua ben Yosef,* to be his Savior. If upright, sincere, generous, dedicated, devout, compassionate, God-fearing living were enough, then Cornelius already had enough to save him. But he still needed Jesus. And Peter was God's chosen way of introducing Jesus to him and to his whole household as their Savior.

This encounter is so crucial to the development of the early church that Acts essentially tells the whole story twice over from chapter 10 to chapter 11. This is a watershed moment for the church and, indeed, for God's whole dealings with humanity. The time for cultural exclusivity had passed. The cultural direction of God's plan turned 180 degrees, from a *centripetal* (inward) trajectory to a *centrifugal* (outward) one. In the centripetal phase God started with a fallen world and went about showing that *some things* could be sanctified. This early approach involved mostly one particular people and its culture, and a dependence on a great deal of rule-keeping and human effort (which is the kind of approach we humans seem to find most natural). (After manifestly demonstrating the limitations of such an approach, God went on to the centrifugal phase, where it would become clear that *all things* could be sanctified, to include all peoples and cultures.) This required no less than Jesus' incarnation, crucifixion, resurrection, and promise to return to make all things new. This is the Good News Peter was sent to declare to Cornelius.

In the course of time, with the passing of eras and the migration of peoples, the culturally centrifugal direction of the gospel would encounter something called ANA culture. And if Peter were sent today to share the Good News about Jesus in an ANA home, he would come in; take his shoes off; perhaps be served tea; have young children in the house call him "Uncle" or "Teacher"; eat with thanksgiving the udon noodles, phõ, roast duck, kim chee, rice porridge, lumpia, or whatever else was served him; and embrace that setting as a fully worthy place for God to give the gift of saving faith in Jesus.

Settling the Question

By the time of the Jerusalem Council in Acts 15, the whole issue of culture and conversion had come to a head. The almost completely Jewish character of the early church—Jewish believers following a Jewish Savior in Jewish settings—had been challenged by the increasing numbers of Gentile believers. The Jewish leaders of the church in Jerusalem were tenuously situated, surrounded by deep-seated, widespread resentment toward Roman rule and all things Gentile. To be increasingly associated with Gentiles presented all manner of problems. It was a major impediment to Jewish evangelization. Would any pious Jews want to be identified with Gentiles who knew nothing of the law and were not being asked to learn and keep it?

Would the Jewish leadership even tolerate such Gentile encroachments?

Jesus had opened the door to reconsidering Mosaic food laws and Sabbath restrictions, and had taught directly about sexual ethics, but he had not left guidance or instructions about matters such as circumcision. The heart of the debate was this question: after the coming of Jesus, was the law of Moses, and especially the requirement of circumcision, still binding? Would Gentiles be welcomed into the church as they had always been welcomed into the Jewish faith: through circumcision and obedience to the law? As the early church attracted more and more Gentiles to faith in Jesus, this was as practical, pressing, and sensitive a matter as could be.

After much research and debate, the Jerusalem Council took the extremely risky route of deciding that circumcision would now *not* be a requirement. Followers of Jesus did not have to keep the law of Moses the way Jews did before the time of Jesus. James, apparently the leader of the Council, concluded, "…we should not make it difficult for the Gentiles who are turning to God" (Acts 15:19, NIV).

The full decision of the Council retained a few points of the law of Moses, for instance, still prohibiting the eating of blood. In the balance of the whole experience of the early church as it unfolds in Scripture, this handful of retained points of the law seems to have been a carefully drawn short list that was small enough not to be burdensome but significant enough to avoid unnecessary offense. This was nevertheless a huge departure from past Jewish belief and practice. At least in principle, the law of Moses had always been taken as a whole. It was all God-given and all to be obeyed. The law was a whole cloth, from the Ten Commandments, to the prohibitions against usury, to the regulations concerning shellfish. In light of Jesus, however, a new principle was established here: even a previously central provision of the law such as circumcision was no longer binding. Lifting this central ritual requirement of the law went to the very heart of cultural matters of identity. One cannot overstate how astonishing and radical this was.

The Council's decision to waive the requirement of circumcision can be taken two ways. A simple (but I believe, erroneous) interpretation of the Council's decision is to take it as meaning that *culture no longer matters*. In this interpretation, things like circumcision, kosher dietary laws, and everything associated with a particular culture—even as "chosen" and privileged a one as Jewish culture in God's redemptive plan—are all now completely irrelevant and useless, if not actually dangerous.

But this is precisely what the Council did not say. The Council *did not forbid circumcision*. There was nothing in the Council's decision to prevent Jewish followers of Jesus from continuing to practice circumcision per their culture and custom. Indeed, there was nothing in the Council's decision to prevent a Gentile follower of Jesus from practicing circumcision. The only thing the Council forbade was *requiring* circumcision as a necessary step toward saving faith in Jesus. Within the Council's decision was the implication, soon to be worked out, that *Gentile culture is acceptable,* this alongside Jewish culture. Thus, the culturally centrifugal trajectory of the gospel is not an abandonment of cultures (even Jewish culture) but an embrace of all cultures.

A Thoroughly Changed Man

If you needed to find someone to effectively propel the spread of Christianity from its Jewish roots into Gentile peoples and settings, you could have hardly found someone less promising than Saul of Tarsus, later known as the apostle Paul. No one would have seemed a worse choice to bridge and cross the cultural chasm between Jew and Gentile. He proudly carried his five-star, bulletproof Jewish pedigree. He was highly educated in the Jewish law and trained to consider even the smallest matters of the law of utmost importance. (This scrupulousness about the law was both religious and patriotic: in the Pharisees' thinking, it was the breaking of this law that had led to the national catastrophes of the Assyrian and Babylonian Captivities, the destruction of the first Temple, and then their conquest by Rome.) He had the personal drive to fully live out his commitments. In short, he was like a Jewish version of the Taliban: absolute, harsh, and completely convinced of the wrongness of any other way of living but his own. He described himself as "circumcised on the eighth day [thus, a cradle Jew and not a later convert], a member of the people of Israel, of the tribe of Benjamin [the same tribe as King Saul, and the location of Jerusalem], a Hebrew born of Hebrews; as to the law, a Pharisee; as to zeal, a persecutor of the church; as to righteousness under the law, blameless" (Philippians 3:5-6).

This same Paul would go on to declare himself "the apostle to the Gentiles" (Romans 11:13, NIV) and to spend the bulk of his career on church-planting work among Gentiles. Early in his apostleship, he directly confronted the then still-unsettled debate over circumcision, staking out what would ultimately become the Council's position. He spent his time on the road adapting to the culture of whomever he was seeking to reach with the gospel, observing or not observing kosher food restrictions, switching languages, selecting different cultural references in his preaching, and circulating both in synagogues and Gentile public settings. He wrote, "I have become all things to all people, that I might by all means save some" (1 Corinthians 9:22).

As with the decision of the Jerusalem Council, there are two ways to take Paul's transformation. One is to think he simply abandoned matters of culture because they no longer mattered; "neither circumcision nor uncircumcision is anything" (Galatians 6:15). The other is to think he still embraced his and others' cultural identities but approached them in a new way. This seems far more likely, for he fully asserted his solidarity with his fellow Jews as "my own people" (Romans 9:3); he did not hesitate to have Timothy circumcised for the sake of further work among Jews, since Timothy's mother (though not his father) was Jewish (Acts 16:3 but, critically, note that Paul adamantly refused to do the same for Titus, who was entirely Gentile [Galatians 2:1-5]). He actively helped and joined others in fulfilling specifically Jewish temple vows (Acts 21:17-26) and personally fulfilled such a vow himself (Acts 18:18). In his various apologias he specifically cited and detailed his Jewish credentials and traditional Jewish observances (e.g., Acts 24). Paul never rejected or renounced his Jewishness. Rather, he added to his Jewishness the ability to adapt to all manner of Gentile people and settings.

At one point, to be Jewish was to be exclusively, even prejudicially, Jewish. God *had* indeed chosen one particular people through whom to work and *had* prescribed much of their culture as a way of getting through to them certain basic lessons about sin, sacrifice, faith, justice, and mercy. God *had* given them stern prohibitions about mingling with other peoples. And with the coming of Jesus, certain aspects of that culture were actually done away with, especially the role of temple-based sacrificial offerings mediated by a designated priesthood. But Jewish forms of prayer, food customs, and no doubt everything from music to dress to family structures certainly could and did continue. And now Jews not only could mingle with Gentiles but were commanded to do so. And mingle they did, becoming one in Christ. "For he is our peace, who has made the two one and has destroyed the barrier, the dividing wall of hostility" (Ephesians 2:14, NIV).

This hardly means Jewish and Gentile cultures were discarded. It is the *animosity* between Jews and Gentiles in focus here. The point is that in Christ there is a new equality. Because of this new equality, the former divisions, suspicions, and animosity are eliminated. I do wish the Ephesians text said more about what actually happened in the midst of Jews and Gentiles being reconciled. Whose music got sung? Whose food showed up at church meals? Whose forms of prayer were used? We can guess that the contributions of both cultures were welcome, and that in time the mixing of the two produced additional "third culture" forms and expressions. We can be certain those cultures did not just disappear, somehow replaced by alien culture-less forms.

One could draw an analogy to marriage. As a man and woman become husband and wife, their oneness as a couple does not take away the different "cultures" of their maleness and femaleness. Indeed, over time we may hope that their maleness and femaleness would only be enhanced and deepened in happy and good ways, along with all the different family and cultural backgrounds and different personal histories they each brought to the marriage. Or think of an interracial couple: would the best path to unity for them be abandoning and rejecting their two racial backgrounds? Surely not. It is precisely in the sharing, mutual discovery, and mixing and matching of their cultures that they can draw closer and closer. So it is with Jews and Gentiles as they come to Christ: they are called to become a "diverse unity."

The same spirit is in Paul's words to the church in Galatia, as he addressed the circumcision question. "There is neither Jew nor Greek, slave nor free, male nor female, for you are all one in Christ Jesus" (Galatians 3:28, NIV). The context has to do with standing before God. In the past, the law privileged some (mostly free adult male Jews) over others (mostly women, slaves, and Gentiles) when it came to relating to God. But with the coming of Christ, those differences in privilege had come to an end. The ground before the cross is level. We all come to Christ equally needy, and find ourselves in Christ equally saved.

This famous text is *not* saying all human distinctions no longer matter in any way (as opposed to not mattering only when it comes to relating to God). If we applied these statements in such a blanket and absolute sense, would we, for example, stop having generally different names for boys and girls, or different hairstyles, clothes, and public restroom facilities based on gender?

Would we not speak different languages? Would we not have culturally different music? Obviously not. Paul is not saying such distinctions mean nothing in any and every way. He is only saying such distinctions mean nothing when it comes to our need for Christ and our place in Christ in matters of salvation and redemption. Being "all one in Christ Jesus" has to do with how we honor each other, think about each other, and value each other. It does not mean obliterating our different races, genders, cultures, and backgrounds. The glory of the gospel is how it enables us to be one body even with these many and diverse identities and cultures.

* * * * *

In the end, the cultural trajectory of God's plan is one of centripetal motion before the coming of Christ to centrifugal motion after his coming. And how could it be otherwise if Christ's instruction is to make followers of all peoples, to the ends of the earth? At one time it was Abraham and Sarah's descendants who particularly would be "a light to the nations" (Isaiah 42:6). But in due time even Gentiles themselves could be described as "saints in the light" (Colossians 1:12). And ANA believers and ANA culture share fully in that light.

CHAPTER 3

Asian North America

Currently in the grade school textbook industry in the United States there is a conscious, "politically correct" avoidance of images and depictions that could be taken as stereotypes. No picture of an elderly person can involve a walker or wheelchair. African Americans cannot be shown singing in a gospel choir or playing basketball. Women cannot be depicted as homemakers; and so forth. Of course, there is a laudable motivation here to avoid and even challenge persistent stereotypes and to help undo harm from the past. Yet it presses the question: can any group be characterized in any way?

Clearly there is no place for stereotyping per se: making generalizations about a group in order to devalue and denigrate its members one and all. But what if the intent is to understand and not to devalue? What if the attempt at understanding starts with the perspective of the group being characterized, rather than from an outsider's view? And what if the characterization avoids being restrictive ("They're all like that") but rather is kept in the realm of the relevantly specific and descriptive ("Many who have that particular background tend to highly value _____ ")? Such attempts may be called *archetypes* in contrast to *stereotypes*. This entire book depends on there being ANA archetypes that are legitimate, worthwhile, and helpful for informing the design of worship in ANA settings. This chapter will try to offer some building blocks toward such ANA cultural archetypes.

Welcome to Asian North America

I am approaching "Asian North America" primarily as a culture, not as a place or race. But that culture starts with Asian North Americans (ANAs). Who are they? Taken at face value, an Asian North American is anyone of any Asian ancestry anywhere on the North American continent, from the tip of Greenland all the way down to the Panama–Colombia border. Anyone in North America who individually or ancestrally came from Asia in the past several centuries (that is, during the modern historical era) is, technically, an Asian North American.

However, this book focuses on English-speaking Christians in Canada and the U.S. with cultural roots in East or Southeast Asia. Who, in this sense, is ANA? Here is a list of some of the cultural commonalities that help describe ANA heritage. The actual assortment of items that applies to any given individual or community, and the degree to which a given assortment applies, ranges very widely.

❖ Ancestral names and linguistic roots in the sinosphere (so, those nations that, along with China itself, use or used Chinese characters as at least one system to write their own majority or official languages, thus *kanji* in Japan, *hanja* in Korea, and *Hán tự* in Vietnam)
❖ Confucian social and ethical heritage, especially regarding duty within hierarchical relationships in the family and in society (so, for example, having ancestral language names with the family name before a given name)
❖ Buddhist and Taoist religious heritage and practice
❖ Historic and more recent migrations and settlements within Asia itself (so, for instance, the very many ethnic Chinese populations and communities in Asia but outside of China, such as the large Chinese populations of Thailand, Malaysia, Singapore, and Indonesia; thus, an immigrant from one of those countries could well be an ethnic Chinese)

❖ American colonialism in the Pacific, especially in the Philippines and numerous Pacific islands

❖ Legal anti-immigration exclusion and discrimination in the mid-nineteenth to mid-twentieth centuries, including wartime internment or forced resettlement of Japanese Americans and Japanese Canadians during World War II

❖ The American Immigration and Nationality (Hart-Cellar) Act of 1965 and the Canadian Immigration Act of 1976, which ended the era of highly restrictive immigration and led to large new migrations from Asia to North America

❖ The American war in Vietnam and surrounding countries and its aftermath, especially trans-Pacific refugee resettlement from Vietnam, Cambodia, and Laos, sometimes via intermediary countries such as Thailand

❖ Being a visible racial minority in the "yellow"/"brown" range, with black hair and brown eyes

❖ Chopsticks as ordinary rather than foreign when used at home (though with exceptions, e.g., Thai cuisine is customarily eaten with fork and spoon)

The purpose of such a wide-ranging list is to try to broadly describe what the ANA population shares, either directly (as in, this is my own experience) or indirectly (as in, this is the experience of a lot of people I know or encounter, and who look like me). The particular assortment, degree, and association for a given individual, family, or cohort might be fractional and even quite conflicted or unwanted, but it is there. The challenge is to list a sufficiently specific cluster of commonalities to provide a useful sense of description, without attempting to be definitive or restrictive.

To focus on English-speaking Christians with cultural roots in East or Southeast Asian means I am neglecting at least five groups, all of them important and absolutely deserving of their own full attention and care along these same lines, but who are outside the scope of this book:

1. *Those of South Asian ancestry, particularly from India, Pakistan, Bangladesh, and Sri Lanka.* On one hand, South Asians often have many commonalities with East and Southeast Asians: a sense of ancient ancestral culture that remains still very much alive today; family-centric, age-honoring, education-esteeming values; a visible immigrant class of shopkeepers; association with non-Christian majority religions (Hinduism, Buddhism, Islam); and live issues of immigration and family sponsorship.

On the other hand, there are substantial differences between South Asians and East/Southeast Asians: mostly very different experiences with colonialism; different immigration histories; largely distinct religious and philosophical roots (excepting Buddhist origins in the subcontinent, and the spread of Islam into Indonesia and Malaysia); and the widespread prominence of English in South Asia, especially in higher education, law, and business (comparable only in other former British and American colonies in Asia, such as Burma [Myanmar], Malaysia, Singapore, Hong Kong, and the Philippines).

By demographics, presence, and influence, South Asians are prominent in Canada in a way that is not presently the case in the U.S. Currently there are slightly more South Asians (taken all together) in Canada than Chinese (who are by far the largest single Asian ancestry in Canada, so that South Asians and Chinese together make up about two-thirds of all Asian Canadians). This South Asian prominence relates to the history of the British Empire and migrations within it. Thus, when one says "Asian" in Canada, one readily and even immediately thinks of someone South Asian (or Chinese), whereas in the U.S. "Asian" usually first brings to mind someone East Asian.

The question then is whether Canadians of East and Southeast Asian ancestry identify with Asian Americans south of the border, perhaps in some ways more so than with fellow Canadians who are South Asian. For the purposes of this book, I am assuming yes, that there is a shared East and Southeast Asian culture that is readily cross-border and legitimate to distinguish from South Asian culture both in Canada and the United States.

2. *Native Hawaiians and Pacific Islanders.* There is a long history now of including these ancestries alongside "Asians," either implicitly or explicitly ("Asian/Pacific Islander," "API"). These ancestries are commonly divided into three groups: Polynesian (including Hawaiian, Samoan, Tahitian, Tongan, and Maori), Micronesian (including Guamanian/Chamorro), and Melanesian (including Fijian). While there has been some shared history with East and Southeast Asians (particularly via migrations and inter-marriage on the Hawaiian Islands), these island peoples really have their own distinct histories and cultures.

3. *Immigrant Asians who continue to identify primarily with their lands of origin.* We often use a shortcut of "Canadian-born" or "American-born" to distinguish native from immigrant Canadian and American Asians, but it is a fairly crude shortcut. Many who are born overseas come to North America and become fully bilingual and bicultural. Others with the exact same background remain exclusive speakers of their ancestral language their entire lives, and have no aspirations to become particularly bicultural. I have relatives like this, who have been in America for decades and still speak Chinese exclusively. Aptitude, circumstances, opportunity, personality, and choice are different for everyone. In any case, immigrant Asian worship settings involve quite different cultural considerations than ANA worship settings, starting most obviously with matters of language. The two do need each other—as long as immigration continues, there will be a need for classic multigenerational bilingual churches, with first-generation immigrants in one congregation and later generations in another. Immigrant ministries remain the future and not just the past. All the questions I am raising in this book are relevant to worship in non-English-speaking immigrant congregations, but pursuing those questions will involve a quite different conversation. May both conversations flourish and may they find ways to help each other. Meanwhile, this book is focused on the English-speaking ANA conversation.

4. *Spanish-speaking Asians in Mexico, Central America, and the Caribbean.* Their numbers and presence are very much smaller, typically no more than a few tens of thousands at most in any given country, with the exceptions of Filipinos in Mexico and Chinese in Panama (with each number around 200,000), plus Chinese in Cuba (around 100,000). In South America there are around 1.3 million Chinese in Peru (along with the much smaller Japanese population that produced former Peruvian President Alberto Fujimori). It remains to be seen if a Spanish-speaking pan-Asian culture will emerge, this alongside some 1.5 million Portuguese-speaking Asian Brazilians (1.4 million of them Japanese).

5. *North, Central, and West Asians* (who are generally considered Caucasian within a North American context). *North* Asia is the Asian portion of Russia (usually taken as the area east of the Ural Mountains), dominated by Siberia. *Central* Asia is Kazakhstan, Kyrgyzstan, Tajikistan, Turkmenistan, and Uzbekistan, all former Soviet Republics; sometimes Afghanistan is also included here. *West* Asia ranges from Iran to Turkey, and south through the entire Arabian peninsula; this area was more commonly known as the Near East or Middle East. While the Silk Road historically provided a connection between West, Central, and East Asia, their histories, languages, and cultures are very distinct.

In naming these five groups that are not the focus of this exploration, I am trying simply to be honest about the cultural landscape and distinctions that are relevant to this particular exploration. I certainly don't mean those distinctions to be guarded boundaries—the next chapter includes a discussion of the need for all worship traditions to engage cultures other than their own, even though doing so is very hard work. But any discussion of as huge a group as "Asians" is going to involve groups with all different amounts of cultural distance between them. We all need different conversations in different rooms (though hopefully each with its door open).

As with categories and labels generally, there are always good reasons to "lump" together and to "split" apart. These remain ever in tension, with the pendulum sometimes swinging one way and sometimes the other. This book proposes that there is a useful lumping of English-speaking Christians of East and Southeast Asian ancestry, in distinction to the five other Asian groups just listed (and many smaller groups), and in distinction to the Canadian and U.S. majority cultures.

A Sense of the Censuses

For both Canada and the United States, the national census includes tabulations of ethnicity and race. Both nations practice self-identification: it's up to each respondent to choose what ethnicity or race to report. It would actually take quite a lengthy and involved presentation to analyze the history and practice of the definitions used and the trends in reported numbers. (There are links in the Resources section at the back of this book.) However, we can attempt a brief description.

The Canadian Census
In the Canadian federal government, the standalone agency Statistics Canada conducts the national census every five years, to include the most recently completed one in 2006 and the one being processed as I write this in 2011. (Unfortunately the actual 2011 data releases will not begin until early 2012, after this book has gone to print. Data on ethnicity are projected to become available in late 2012.) Respondents indicate one of the suggested ethnic origins (e.g., White, Chinese, South Asian, Latin American) or write one in, and they may indicate more than one. Starting with the Employment Equity Act of 1995, Canada also

makes widespread use of the category of "visible minority," which is defined as "persons, other than aboriginal peoples, who are non-Caucasian in race or non-white in colour." Per this definition, the main categories of visible minorities are, in descending order of population in 2006: Chinese, South Asian, Black, Filipino, Latin American, Southeast Asian, Arab, West Asian, Korean, and Japanese. (Note that this differs at several points from the race categories used in the United States census.)

Altogether, the 2006 count reported just over 5 million visible minority persons, of whom 3.5 million were all varieties of Asian, out of a total Canadian population of 31.2 million. Among Asian Canadians, 1.3 million were South Asian (just under 1 million of them East Indian), and 2.2 million were East and Southeast Asian. (These numbers are "total responses" including those who identified as more than one ethnic origin.) Of the 2.2 million East and Southeast Asian Canadians, the largest groups were Chinese (1.35 million), Filipino (0.44 million), Vietnamese (0.18 million), Korean (0.15 million), and Japanese (0.10 million). At the most general level, all Asian Canadians taken together are Canada's largest visible minority, comprising about 11.3 percent of the population (compared with around 5.6 percent for Asian Americans).

The United States Census

The United States Census Bureau (part of the Department of Commerce) conducts its count every ten years. Its definitions of ethnicity and race are provided by the Office of Management and Budget. In the 1980 and 1990 counts, "Asian or Pacific Islander" was one of the races one could choose. In the 2000 count, "Asian" was separated from "Native Hawaiian or Other Pacific Islander" and, for the first time ever, respondents could mark more than one race. The 2010 count followed the 2000 definitions. Results are tabulated in five major race categories (White, Black, Asian, American Indian or Alaska Native, and

Native Hawaiian or Other Pacific Islander) and many secondary categories of specific ethnic and national origins. By the Census definition, one can be of Hispanic or Latino Origin and be of any race; on the Census form the "Hispanic or Latino Origin" question is separate from the "Race" question. (A little over half of those who identify as Hispanic or Latino identify racially as "white"; a little over a third identify as "some other race.") Notably in the 2000 and 2010 counts, separate tabulations are available for "Taiwanese."

The national 2010 data have just begun to be released as I write this (September 2011). For those identifying as one race only, the largest Asian groups were Chinese (3.35 million), Asian Indian (2.84 million), Filipino (2.56 million), Vietnamese (1.55 million), Korean (1.42 million), and Japanese (0.76 million). Taken all together, there were 14.7 million (4.8 percent of the population) who identified as Asian alone and 17.3 million (5.6 percent of the population) as Asian and one or more other races. (Note that someone who is, say, Chinese and Cambodian would still be "Asian alone.") From 2000 to 2010, Asians were the fastest-growing race by percentage change, increasing 43.3 percent (for Asian alone), against a total rise in population of 9.7 percent.

Both the Canadian and U.S. census websites are first-rate and highly interactive (see links in the "Resources" section in the back of this book). They provide population figures sliced virtually any way you would like, for both characteristics (age, gender, race and ethnicity, etc.) and geography (from local to national). You can learn, for instance, that in 2006, of the 1.2 million Canadian Chinese (here, Chinese alone), 310,085 were Canadian born and 870,955 were immigrants. You can learn that my block (Block 2001, Census Tract 4049, Alameda County, California) is 15.8 percent Asian. As the complete data for both nations' most recent counts become available into 2012, it will be fascinating to examine the numbers in full detail, especially for groups with currently high immigration rates.

Both Canada and the United States use census data on race and ethnicity primarily to enforce their various antidiscrimination laws involving education, employment, housing, and political representation. As our nations take great care and expense to be just in educational, economic, and political opportunities, we can likewise use such data to inform our own callings to reach every corner of the ANA community. This will include creating worship settings that, taken together, provide a warm welcome to every different flavor of ANA and convey that the gospel is for each of them too.

On Becoming "Asian"

If you asked my own parents what ethnicity they are, they (both American-born descendents of immigrants from the Guangdong province of southern China) would likely say "Chinese" and not "Asian." The idea of a collective Asian disaporic identity is quite recent and still fairly early in formation. The term "Asian American" was first coined by Yuji Ichioka (1936–2002), who taught history at the University of California, Los Angeles. Ichioka was a Japanese American WWII internment camp survivor who went on to help organize the Asian American Political Alliance at the University of California, Berkeley in the 1960s. This was the first group to identify itself as Asian American. The term "Asian American" not only displaced the older colonial-era terms "Oriental" and "Asiatic" but helped build new bonds between those of Chinese, Japanese, Filipino, Korean, and other ancestries who formerly did not view themselves collectively. "Asian American" also provided an identity that helped cultivate peer-level partnerships with black, Native American, and Hispanic/Latino groups in an overall effort at racial minority empowerment.

After immigration reform in the United States and Canada in the 1960s and 1970s, the door was open for the first time in decades for large-scale Asian immigration, leading to much family unification but still favoring advanced students, those who brought business assets, or those with high-level education and skills. Those were the post-war years for Korea (though technically the war has still not ended to this day), with its primary U.S. involvement and subsequent migrations, and much smaller but still significant volunteer Canadian involvement in the United Nations forces under U.S. command. Then came the peak and ending years of the U.S. war in Southeast Asia and the resulting exodus of many Vietnamese (including many ethnic Vietnamese, Chinese from Vietnam, and minority groups that were United States allies, such as the Hmong); the Killing Fields in Cambodia and the resulting stream of refugees to places like Thailand and then some to North America; the 1997 transfer of Hong Kong from the British back to the People's Republic of China; and the economic booms of Japan in the 1980s, the "Tiger Economies" of the '90s (South Korea, Hong Kong, Taiwan, and Singapore), and the current ascendancy of Mainland China.

In my own lifetime, the Chinatown of my hometown, Oakland, California, has gone from a Taishan-heavy enclave of working-class Cantonese Chinese, to a much more poly-Chinese community with the arrival of many Fukienese and then Mainland Chinese, to a quite pan-Asian setting with the arrival of Vietnamese (both ethnic Vietnamese and ethnic Chinese), Cambodians, and other Southeast Asians, with a growing Koreatown not far away. In the 1980s my own father-in-law, Jack Wong, helped start the Five Counties association in Oakland, which was the first such association in America to recognize the People's Republic of China (in what had long been a reliably Taiwan-loyal setting). I have now lived long enough to have seen a feature movie with an array of Asian American characters whose particular ancestries (Chinese? Japanese? Korean?) were largely unspecified and more or less irrelevant (Justin Lin's 2002 film *Better Luck Tomorrow*). Year by year, decade by decade, the sense of being ANA continues to evolve and change.

From There, From Here

Very roughly speaking, one can generalize Asian North Americans into three groups based on immigration histories: (1) those who had a substantial past immigration history going back to the nineteenth century, but whose immigration rates have since largely tapered off (e.g., Japanese); (2) those who had such a history and still have ongoing high levels of immigration (e.g., Chinese, Filipino); and (3) those whose major immigration only began in the later twentieth century and are still ongoing (e.g., Korean, Southeast Asian). Thus, there are relatively few Japanese-speaking *issei* congregations anymore in North America, and very high outmarriage rates to non-Japanese. In contrast, though Chinese have been in North America in substantial numbers for five and more generations, the majority of Chinese here continues to be first-generation. (Partly this is due to the severe declines in natural and immigration growth during the exclusion decades in both Canada and the United States, without which there would be substantially more multi-generational Chinese North Americans today.) Meanwhile, Southeast Asians are just now seeing large numbers of their first North American–born generation come of age and begin to establish themselves in their professional, community, and public lives.

One may say generally that Canada is more used to openly, officially, and actively working on multicultural issues right up to the highest levels. Because of this, paradoxically there is often less "political correctness" in discussions, because boundaries are already clear. For example, Canada has two official languages, English and French, so the issue of national language is settled (at least in policy; only New Brunswick is truly demographically bilingual). In contrast, while English clearly dominates in the U.S., it is not the legally official language, and so the matter is an endless source of debate, touchiness, polarization, confusion, and posturing.

At the same time, the idea of a collective Asian identity is much more prominent in America than in Canada. One is more likely to hear "CBC" (Canadian-born Chinese) than "Asian Canadian," whereas one is now more likely to hear "Asian American" than "ABC" (American-born Chinese). Partly this is due to sheer demographics and immigration history (Chinese dominating Asian Canadians in a way *no* national or ethnic group dominates Asian Americans). But perhaps this is also partly because Canadian multiculturalism is more defined and accepted, and therefore not as needful of new or modified categories.

As a whole, ANA culture is not something fully developed, expressed, and understood. It is not like a mature tree full of expressed shape and character. Rather, ANA culture is like a seedling or perhaps a sapling, full of life and potential but very far from having taken its mature shape. We may press the analogy a bit further to say there is no guarantee ANA culture will grow to take on a mature shape—that depends on myriad choices that could lead one way or another.

On the extremes, ANA could either become just a minor variety of the majority culture, or it could become an aggressively defiant counter to the majority. More likely of course it will settle into a range somewhere in between these extremes. By comparison one can think of, say, Irish North Americans, who have some ancestral affinities (St. Patrick's Day! Notre Dame!) but have largely assimilated into the white majority. Compare the Irish to Jewish North Americans, who are also considered white, but many of whom have sustained a remarkably distinct and full parallel identity and culture. Compare the Irish and Jews to, say, African Americans, who are the most visible minority (to borrow the Canadian term) and also have a heritage of something approaching a full and distinct parallel identity and culture (though this has become even more complex over time). Which will ANAs become more like in the future?

Here are some adjectives to help navigate ANA culture. *Emergent*: "Newly coming into view, existence or notice." *Delitescent*: "Not easily seen, concealed." *Latent*: "Present with potential but not fully developed or active." These are not negative labels but simply descriptions of where ANA culture stands as the product of both ancient ancestral roots an ocean away and really quite recent historical developments.

Meanwhile, all cultures are complex and ever-changing. Not even a century ago, the U.S. racial category of "white" did not include groups such as those with Irish or Jewish ancestry. Not very long ago, it would have been unimaginable for a deceased African American woman to lie in state in the United States Capitol Rotunda—but that is what happened to Rosa Parks in 2005. And now we have our first African American president of the United States, something so many never thought they would live to see. Perhaps it would be easier in some ways for ANAs to have a culture that is not so relatively young and still in formation. (On the other hand, working with an emergent, delitescent, latent culture gives us relatively more freedom to shape the future rather than perpetuating the past.) (In Chapter 5 I will explore further the challenges of identifying with a young culture.)

On Being a Bicultural Minority

My neighborhood where I live has a pretty robust e-mail group with a couple thousand subscribers. I remember once a neighbor posting an urgent request for last-minute babysitting help — the couple had big plans for that very night and their childcare had fallen through. Might any neighbor be available? My wife and I laughed and shook our heads. An open invitation for a *stranger* to watch one's children? Apart from everything else one might say about such a request, it is a majority-culture move, only possible to the degree that these neighbors thought of the neighborhood as "us." In the same way, friends tell me that in Seoul you will routinely see young children alone on the subway; this in no small part because South Korea has one of the most homogeneous populations of any nation today. Everyone on the train is "us." These are both monocultural majority examples of identity.

To be ANA is to be both bicultural and a cultural minority. And to be bicultural is further complicated because biculturality includes different combinations of cultures. Generally speaking a given individual may have less or greater fluency and attachment to ancestral culture, and less or greater fluency to North American majority culture. Some are truly bicultural, speaking ancestral and majority languages, knowledgeable about the holidays and customs of both cultures, able to explain and translate each culture to the other, and perhaps able to be a "local" both here and when traveling in their homelands. Some are still mostly rooted in ancestral culture, almost like a group of tourists in North America, never really identifying with the majority culture. Some identify almost entirely with the majority culture and are thus considered "assimilated."

And there are some who do not identify strongly with either ancestral or majority culture, perhaps because of immigrating at an awkward age (say, mid-teens) and not having the aptitude to adapt well. Such people are alienated from both cultures and don't feel entirely at home in either. Each of these variations of biculturality is its own subculture, and each will bring different needs and gifts into worship settings. (We can also note that everyone has a shot at helping shape the majority culture. One of my hopes is that ANA worship can do that very thing.) So, even within the minority culture that is ANA culture as a whole, there are these further subcultures that may, in a given setting, be minorities of minorities. And these deserve to be noticed and valued in the same way that ANA culture as a whole seeks to be noticed and valued within the majority culture.

East Meets West

It is common to think of ANA biculturality as a set of contrasts between east and west. These contrasts are rooted in their differing cultural sources. Eastern sources include Confucius (*ren* "humanity," and having inherited relationships with inherited duties); Taoism ("yin/yang" paradoxical balance, *wu wei* "action through nonaction," and the *Tao* "Way"); and Buddhism (suffering as attachment, impermanence, karma, reincarnation, and enlightenment). Western sources include Judeo-Christian roots (rule of law, value of individual, possibility of redemption), Greco-Roman roots (reason, dialog, inquiry, democracy), and American roots (political freedom, individualism, social mobility, self-definition, and self-reinvention). These differing sources underlie differing ways of approaching life and of being, such as the following examples:

A. Personal Bearing and Interaction Style
Reticent, reserved, restrained
    versus forthcoming, expressive, demonstrative
Indirect, implicit, subtle, non-confrontational
    versus direct, explicit, straightforward, confrontational
Self-effacing, -deprecating, -sacrificing
    versus self-promoting, -affirming, -referring
Knowing more than you say
    versus saying more than you know
Deferential, authority-accepting, idealization of maturity
    versus confrontational, authority-challenging, idealization
    of youthfulness
Risk-adverse, reactive, responsive
    versus risk-taking, proactive, aggressive

B. Relation of Self to Group
Inherited, hierarchical relationships
    versus voluntary, egalitarian relationships
Family = primary social unit
    versus individual = primary social unit
Enduring attachment to parents
    versus early separation from parents

Group harmony paramount
   versus individual success paramount
Rise to obligation, duty, responsibility
   versus rise to freedom, liberty, rights
Avoids shame, loss of face
   versus avoids lost opportunity, loss of fame
Honor through conformity ("The nail that sticks up gets hammered down")
   versus honor through individualism ("I did it my way")

C. Philosophical Bent
Reflective and meditative
   versus analytical and active
Narrative, story, experience
   versus proposition, fact, concept
Cyclical, paradoxical
   versus linear, logical
Faith in tradition, wisdom
   versus faith in progress, knowledge
Acceptance of tragedy and suffering
   versus need to avoid or fix tragedy and suffering
Long historical memory
   versus short historical memory

So, for instance, to be reserved and deferential may not be signs of timidity and inability but rather a tradition of hierarchical relationships (wait until whoever is in charge asks you to speak), *wu wei* (saying less, not more, often accomplishes more—which agrees with James 1:19!), and *ren* (one's humanity toward others is shown by deferring to them). Surely such contrasts, tensions, and differing perspectives greatly shape our sensibilities as we go to church on Sunday. Surely it does not help to assume that the western forms and values that were the "package" through which the ANA church has mostly encountered Christianity are in fact simply Christian forms and values. Surely the ANA church needs to specially explore and embrace the eastern side of its biculturality—both because it is so much of who we are, and because no one else will or should do that for us.

The Gifts and Challenges of Biculturality

I would like to think that being bicultural means we can affirm the best of both sides of these characteristics. So much of faith and worship involves a balance of truths and realities in tension: suffering and celebration, immanence and transcendence, truth and mystery. Surely one of the gifts of being bicultural is our access to a wider range of cultural understandings and impulses with which to help shape our worship lives.

I think of Yao Ming's early years playing for the Houston Rockets and the talk of having to teach him more of a "killer instinct" if he were to survive in the United States's National Basketball Association. Now that he is retired, we may hope he both benefited from the best that western basketball has to offer and also made his own contributions to the sport from his eastern roots and upbringing. I think of our Christian calling to find our lives by losing them, to experience joy through suffering, to worship God who is one yet three, and to follow Jesus who is our friend but also the King of kings and Lord of lords. Surely an eastern capacity to live with paradox and suffering (rather than the western sense of needing everything to be clear and fixed) can be an asset. "I want to know Christ and the power of his resurrection and the sharing of his sufferings by becoming like him in his death" (Philippians 3:10). Western culture is generally not very interested in sharing in anyone's sufferings. We might be happy to help fix others' sufferings, preferably quickly. But to share in sufferings that do not simply get fixed—we can learn that more from eastern culture.

At the same time, to be a bicultural minority is to live in uncertainty and tension. On the one hand, people who choose to identify themselves as belonging to a minority group (whether racial or otherwise) do not want to be simply assimilated, to be treated as "honorary white." On the other hand, they do want to fit in, to not be treated as "forever foreigner." This sets up what W. E. B. Du Bois memorably deemed a "double-consciousness" in his landmark 1903 essay, "Of Our Spiritual Strivings":

> After the Egyptian and Indian, the Greek and Roman, the Teuton and Mongolian, the Negro is a sort of seventh son, born with a veil, and gifted with second-sight in this American world,—a world which yields him no true self-consciousness, but only lets him see himself through the revelation of the other world. It is a peculiar sensation, this double-consciousness, this sense of always looking at one's self through the eyes of others, of measuring one's soul by the tape of a world that looks on in amused contempt and pity. One ever feels his twoness,—an American, a Negro; two souls, two thoughts, two unreconciled strivings; two warring ideals in one dark body, whose dogged strength alone keeps it from being torn asunder. The history of the American Negro is the history of this strife,—this longing to attain self-conscious manhood, to merge his double self into a better and truer self....

So it is for ANAs, never far from having to live life half managing others' expectations and perceptions, both wanting and not wanting to represent ANAs in general, and never quite sure where to fit in. Although there has been a definite uptick of "regular" Asian lead roles in the media, it is still not only possible but routine for other Asian characters to be depicted as "forever foreigners." Usually they are heavily accented (if speaking English at all) and depicted as manifestly foreign figures. The 2006 American Academy Award winner for Best Picture, *Crash*, was explicitly structured around matters of race and culture. It included a wide range of characters of many different races depicted as complex characters capable of both good and evil. But the Asian characters included stereotypes such as the soulless human trafficker, the shrieking dragon lady, the robotic bureaucrat, and a van full of mute, uneducated, stowaway immigrants.

Or to cite another example, the very title of 2007's *The Pursuit for Happyness* is a "forever foreigner" depiction. In the movie, the misspelled "Happyness" is taken from the name of a fictional preschool set in San Francisco's Chinatown. In the scene where the lead character, played by Will Smith, points out this misspelling to a worker at the preschool, he simply receives an earful of dismissive Cantonese. The orthographically challenged preschool staff are the only Asians depicted in the film—this in a film set in a city with the largest Chinatown outside Asia, and a large Asian American population well over a century old by the early 1980s, the time depicted in the movie.

Surely there are plenty of Asian Americans in San Francisco working at the kind of financial firms that are at the center of this film's plot—but you do not see them depicted here. Even in such a setting, the big-budget, mainstream, star-led movie perpetuated a "forever foreigner" ANA identity. The question is not whether immigrants from non-English-speaking cultures have a hard time with standard English—many obviously do, alongside any number of American-born, American-educated high school graduates. The question is how much a "forever foreigner" cultural identity continues to be perpetuated.

The examples continue to flow freely. In 2011 we had two national-headline-ranking dust-ups: the reaction to Amy Chua's *Battle Hymn of the Tiger Mother* (or, perhaps more accurately, the reaction to the *Wall Street Journal*'s January 8, 2011, headline "Why Chinese Mothers Are Superior" for a story on Chua's book), and the YouTube video battle over former University of California, Los Angeles student Alexandra Wallace's "Asians in the Library" rant. What is the church saying or doing that helpfully responds to such contretemps? What happens in our Sunday worship services that is relevant to the tensions within and around our bicultural identities?

Being bicultural, we live with the majority culture, with ancestral culture(s), with the bicultural mix of the two, and with other minority cultures around us. There will always be a sense of displacement and alienation with such a mix. There will always be reasons to continue to ask: Who am I? Who are we? Yet even this can be an asset in living out our Christian calling as exiles and aliens (1 Peter 1:17; 2:11), that is, as a people who can make their home anywhere in the world, and yet never be truly home anywhere in this world.

A Voice from the True North

I'm guessing that the majority of those picking up this book are Asian Americans like me. To help us further in getting to know our neighbors to the north, let me share a dialog I had with Greer Anne Wenh-In Ng, a pastor and professor emerita at Emmanuel College, the University of Toronto, Ontario. She is also the author of the essay "The Asian North American Community at Worship: Issues of Indigenization and Contextualization" in *People on the Way*, the "prequel" to this book (see more in the Introduction), as well as many other journal articles and book chapters. Of course it is always tricky asking any one person to speak for a whole people. (How many times have many of us been put in that position, awkwardly being asked to give the "Asian" view of something?) However, I think you will find it worth balancing my Asian American voice with a first-person Asian Canadian voice. (Note that several of these questions anticipate later chapters in this book.)

Q: What are some of the more important things Asian Americans should know about Asian Canadians?
For starters, Canada continues to be a member of the (British) Commonwealth, with Her Majesty Queen Elizabeth II as its official

monarch, despite its independent "dominion" status since 1867. Besides its two European "founding nations," the French and the British, dominant Canada is very much aware of its Native Aboriginal/First Nations plus Métis (French-Native descendents) and Inuit ("Eskimo" in American parlance) populations and is sensitive to the nation's colonial history with them, including its present-day consequences (rather than, for instance, the central place of the history of slavery and its consequences in the United States).

So, in Canada there is no primary white-black divide, but rather an evolving dominant-nondominant dynamic brought about by its waves of immigration since after the First World War (Eastern European, Irish, and then Southern European) to the present day (East, South, and Southeast Asians; Caribbean; Sub-Saharan African; and Arabic from western Asia and North Africa), plus sizeable waves of political refugees throughout these periods. Multiculturalism in Canada was officially instituted by a federal government multiculturalism policy in 1971, strengthened by the Charter of Rights and Freedoms in 1982, and further affirmed by the Multicultural Act of 1988.

Q: What are some particular gifts your culture brings to worship?
Gifts that Asian cultures, and in my case specifically Chinese culture, can bring to enrich their Christian worship practices could include music, including the use of traditional instruments as well as indigenous hymnody; meaningful symbols and art (such as Chinese couplets in banner form on red paper in brush calligraphy that incorporate Christian-oriented Lunar New Year greetings); mining creation myths, folk tales, and wisdom sayings as well as the classics for interpreting Scripture and for use in sermons and prayers; and imbuing traditional festivals with Christian connections and meaning to enable church members to be well-integrated holistic beings, strong in both their Christian and cultural identities. *[Author Note: See some of her articles on this subject, listed in the Resources section of this book.]*

One additional way minority Asian cultures can contribute to Christian worship is by developing prayers and rituals to mark life milestones special to these cultures (full-month and sixtieth birthday celebrations, anniversaries of the death of loved ones), plus occasions special to migration activities such as families or individuals saying goodbye to home and home country, blessing the first day at school or work in the new host country, etc.

Q: Many say that all churches should be multicultural in order to best reflect God's kingdom. How would you respond? What is the place of minority culture churches? How do you navigate the relationship between minority and majority cultures?

As long as there are first-generation immigrants needing faith communities that function in their mother tongue, and as long as racial discrimination continues to exist on this continent, minority culture or ethnic minority churches will continue to have a place. Even in denominations that have made public commitments to multicultural or intercultural ministries (the Presbyterian Church USA among the former, The United Church of Canada among the latter), minority culture and language-specific churches (other than English!) are necessary not only to provide safe spaces where communication and support are possible, but also where first-generation immigrants can make decisions without always being marginalized.

Q: How would you describe the current generational dynamics in churches from your culture? How is multigenerational worship and generationally targeted worship faring?

My experience in Canada is that services that try to combine generations across language boundaries often turn out to be a euphemism for separate, generationally targeted services. Efforts to include the younger generations may be expressed in a bilingual order of worship, conducting Scripture readings and prayers and announcements in both languages as much as possible, and usually having the sermon interpreted from ancestral language to English. More often than not, the power to plan, decide, and focus still resides with the earlier generation. Even when a congregation is strong enough to afford a "separate but equal" English-speaking worship service with its own clergyperson, such a secondary worshipping group remains part of that congregation and thus often, if not always, assumes a subordinate position.

When this happens, what is left behind or lost is the sense of a large or extended family worshipping together, with children and grandchildren sitting by the side of parents and grandparents, sharing the same faith bound by their cultural identity and heritage. What can be created could be a sense of autonomy or freedom; confidence that comes with ease of communication; the space to plan and make decisions around how worship is done, and thus hopefully to chart out and experience a fresh way of being Christian. In order to recapture or facilitate some of the goals of a larger, extended faith family, and to inculcate a mutual respect for generational and cultural difference, the generations might consider joining together for worship on important festivals of the church year such as Christmas, Thanksgiving, and Easter, or the Sundays closest to celebrations of important cultural festivals such as the Lunar New Year and the mid-autumn/Korean thanksgiving festivals.

Q: Later-generation Christians often perceive ancestral culture as distinctly "old-fashioned" and something belonging to their parents' and grandparents' generations. How have you responded to such diverging cultural trajectories?
Younger generations perceiving the cultures of older generations as old-fashioned and out-of-date applies not only to the later generations of minority culture groups, but to most younger generations in general. Cohorts growing up in similar circumstances, exposed to similar technological, musical, or consumer tastes in contemporary cultures that span the globe these days, naturally share more

with one another than with their parents and grandparents, from preferring guitar to organ, words projected on a screen to the printed page, even more evangelical "nondenominational" praise songs to hymns of a particular Christian faith tradition.

To respond with alarm and disapproval would only widen the gap; to uncritically condone everything youth likes (or is pressured by peers to like) would be irresponsible. A *via media* (middle way) to try might be to offer support while not shirking the responsibility of pointing out some of the dangers and weaknesses to one's faith and life, whether it be worshipping an exclusively male "lord" God or losing the ability to enjoy printed books or to appreciate western civilization's rich sacred music.

Q: How important has it been for (any/some/many) worshippers of your ancestry to find their own voice in Sunday worship—something they recognize as their own? How much has culture mattered to them?

It seems to me that, for most minority culture church members, the question of "voice" pertains more to having a say in retaining the liturgical forms and practices they are comfortable with (the way the elements are distributed and received during Communion, for example) than to striving for some say in consciously claiming or reclaiming a place for cultural elements in their Sunday worship. The way they usually operate is to separate into two compartments their Christian faith allegiance and their cultural customs and practices, to the extent of consciously or unconsciously eliminating the religious dimensions of their original religio-cultures by treating, for instance, traditional festivals such as new year or *Ching Ming* (Chinese spring commemoration of the dead/ancestors) as purely "secular culture" celebrations.

If anything, most members are so indoctrinated into keeping Christian faith and worship practices "pure" that they would need permission to even think of the possibility of "adulterating" Christian worship with elements from their ancestral cultures, never mind claiming their right to do so. In most cases that I am aware of, it would require much assurance and encouragement from pastoral leadership to help them embark on such a daring journey, even if unconsciously they long for it.

Q: Incorporating minority-culture elements in worship may feel cheesy and gimmicky, a kind of "missionary Sunday" effect. How have you minimized or avoided this? Should majority-culture churches try to include minority-culture forms?

To avoid such pitfalls, it is strategic to try incorporating a variety of non-western, minority, and global cultural elements into regular worship all year round, and not confine them to one or two special Sundays such as Worldwide Communion Sunday or a designated "multicultural Sunday." Acting on the recognition of being part of a global church, singing liturgically appropriate hymns from Ghana, South Africa, or Peru, or occasionally praying a Native four-directions prayer can in time become "normal" for culturally diverse worship in both ethnic minority and ethnic majority churches.

For majority culture churches to make special efforts to include minority cultures is a laudable endeavor if motivated by a genuine desire to learn to celebrate "God's world of riotous difference," as Letty Russell puts it, or to try to be equal partners with churches of a variety of cultures. Otherwise, such endeavors can easily become tokenism (wanting to be seen as inclusive and diverse), paternalistic (in the old colonial missionary sense), or self-serving (motivated by the need to increase church membership). Requiring newcomers to conform to existing ways of a particular majority culture faith community without its own members being willing to be themselves transformed does not make for truly respectful intercultural encounters that empower both parties.

On a denominational level, we need liturgical offerings from culturally minority entities of a denomination to be adopted or incorporated into official hymn books or service books, which happens much less frequently than it could and should. This is especially the case for contemporary compositions originating in North America, rather than hymns and prayers already published and in use in Asian churches. These latter occasionally "make it" into denominational hymn and service books in an effort by those denominations to become more globally inclusive, and is a welcome development, helpfully signaling to English-speaking later generations of these cultural minorities of their being included.

Thank you for helping educate those of us south of the border! You're very welcome.

A Reflective Pause

We have so much to learn about each other and from each other simply as ANAs with our differing ancestral backgrounds, generations, and nationalities. We cannot expect others to take a greater interest in us than we take in ourselves—and based on what happens in our churches on Sunday mornings, what level of interest do we seem to have? What justifies having ANA churches beyond the particular needs of the immigrant generation? What keeps ANA churches from just being ethnic enclaves? Without an actual ANA worship tradition, I have to wonder. If we are largely a minor variation on majority-culture worship (specializing in the calmer, more reflective range of praise music), then why go through all the work of having our own churches? (My hope is that the church can be a leader of and an asset to the place that is Asian North America, and that our worship can be a true and beautiful part of that.)

CHAPTER 4

Christ and Culture

No one says all Christian worship should be in Aramaic, or that only first-century Palestinian Jewish music, architecture, and dress are proper for worship. We agree that the language and style of worship should properly be not that of Jesus' first followers but that of all different worshippers in all their various times and places.

Consider that around the world in Muslim Friday prayers, the Qur'an is always read only in Classical Arabic, never in translation. In contrast, in Christian worship the Scriptures are almost always read in translation, and insofar as possible in the most appropriate available vernacular. (English speakers have an embarrassing [some would say scandalous] number of choices when it comes to Bible translations, with endless varieties of reading level, translation philosophy, "political" identity, book design, and more.)

The Christian approach is vastly more laborious than the Muslim one, with hundreds of major languages and thousands of minor languages to serve (many of the minor ones not even having a written tradition). Even deciding what to call God is often a matter of great debate and consideration. Should Arabic-speaking Christians use *Allah* for God? Should they use a modified form, such as *Allāh al-'Ab* ("God the Father")? For Chinese Christians there is a long history and still ongoing translation debate over using the historic *Shangdi* ("high ruler") versus the more generic *Shen* ("spirit," "diety"), alongside other terms such as *Zhu* ("Lord") and *Tianfu* ("Heavenly Father"). The issues are theological (should Christians use a "pre-Christian" term?), historical (is it in fact pre-Christian?), political (Roman Catholic versus Protestant use), linguistic (what are the translation considerations for YHWH?), stylistic, and simply pastoral, which is all to say that major issues of culture permeate even so basic a matter as what to call God.

In shaping and leading worship, there are endless cultural forms and expressions to consider and weigh—everything from music, to forms for the Lord's Table and for baptism, to leadership roles in worship, to architecture and decoration, to gesture and movement, to every ritual action. When I was in seminary in the late 1980s, one major debate was over "seeker-driven" Sunday services, which stressed accessibility to the unchurched and therefore used culturally neutral worship spaces, conversational discourse, television-style presentation forms (short drama pieces in worship), pop music genres, contemporary language Bible translations (NIV and not KJV), and an overall sensibility about people coming as "seekers" and not (yet) believers. Endless ink was spilled at the time debating the legitimacy of such developments. At its heart, the debate was over the relationship of worship to its surrounding culture, which is a subset of the larger question of the relationship of Christ to culture.

In 1996 an international working group from the Lutheran tradition brought several years of study and discussion together in a document that has come to be known as the "Nairobi Statement on Worship and Culture." It set out a simple, balanced, four-fold approach to the relationship between worship and culture and has since become widely used in discussions on the topic. When such discussions become stuck or otherwise unhelpful, it is often because they have dwelled too much on one or another of the four categories rather than using them all side-by-side. The four categories describe worship as *transcultural* (universal), *contextual* (culture-embracing), *counter-cultural* (culture-rejecting), and *cross-cultural* (culture-mixing). Let's take a closer look at these four categories.

Worship Is Transcultural (Universal)

Some aspects of worship will be true and present in all times and places. The object of Christian worship is God as revealed in Jesus Christ, always and everywhere. The church, the body of Christ, is always a missional community of believers and never just a setting for private belief and practice. The current consensus on the basic actions of Christian worship is a four-fold movement: 1. Gathering, 2. Word, 3. Table, and 4. Sending. Within that four-fold movement are expressions of praise, petition, confession and pardon, adoration, thanksgiving, proclamation, instruction, exhortation, and devotion.

We have been given a Trinitarian water ritual of initiation and a table ritual of remembrance and nourishment. We have been given the good news to share of salvation from sin and God's good plans to ultimately fulfill his purposes for us and for all creation, this through Jesus' birth, death, resurrection, and future return as King of kings and Lord of lords. We have been given the Holy Spirit and God's Word on which to build together one church unified across time and space (though Scripture itself is fully human and culturally expressed, along with being fully divine). All this takes on very different forms and expressions in different cultures, but the object of our worship—its sources and its functions, its hopes and effects—is the same for all cultures.

When some worship leaders might say, "Culture doesn't matter, let's just worship the Christian way," perhaps this transcultural aspect of worship is what they have in mind. The rub of course is that transcultural aspects never exist in a vacuum; they can only be experienced in cultural forms. As a parallel, think of the food we eat. Food always comes in culturally defined forms.

You cannot simply eat carbohydrates or proteins; you have to eat baked potatoes or rice or tortillas, meat loaf or chicken chow mein or carne asada. These culturally defined forms of food develop and change over time, often blending into other cultures and becoming part of them. But food always has cultural meanings rooted in its physical properties and people's experiences. Indeed, it is those very cultural forms that give food its appeal and desirable variety. Some years ago, my late father-in-law was taking a course of medicine that greatly diminished his sense of taste, and consequently all his food tasted the same. I have never seen a more unhappy sight than him not (culturally) enjoying a single bite, even though he was getting the same (transcultural) nutrition as always. In the same way, the transcultural aspects of worship are fundamental but they are never encountered apart from culture.

Worship Is Contextual (Culture-Embracing)

All worship involves the cultures of those gathered to worship, using those cultures as a God-given palatte from which to create specially good, God-pleasing offerings of worship. Perhaps the most obvious example of contextualization is the use of everyday languages for prayer and praise. Today we take for granted this use of vernacular languages in worship. However, the use of everyday languages in worship was one of the central issues during the Protestant Reformation and then four centuries later up to the Roman Catholic reforms of Vatican II. Martin Luther himself translated the Bible into German so that it could be read and proclaimed in the vernacular. He was so successful that his translation is still widely used today. He also wrote many new hymns in German (so that the common people, who did not know Latin, could sing them), his most famous one being "A Mighty Fortress" (EIN FESTE BURG).

All this was revolutionary at the time—that the everyday street language and culture of German Christians was worthy for

Christian worship, that what happened in church could and should be contextualized into the everyday world of German peasants, laborers, artisans, and homemakers. We take it for granted now but it was a revolution at the time. Likewise, the Roman Catholic reforms of Vatican II in the 1960s, turning Catholic worship from centuries of fixed, monocultural liturgy in Latin to the full range of the world's languages, was a full-scale revolution. We might even lament some of the more polarizing aspects of the Reformation and Counter Reformation, without which such contextualization would have surely taken place much earlier.

There are many more historical examples of contextualizing worship. Let me share two that offer excellent advice on developing culture-embracing worship. The first involves the reintroduction of Christianity to the British Isles in the late sixth century, and the second involves the evangelization of China and Southeast Asia in the seventeenth century.

A Little Bouquet

In AD 596, Bishop Gregory of Rome (later known as Gregory the Great) sent Augustine, a monk in Rome (later known as Augustine of Canterbury, not to be confused with the earlier theologian and church father Augustine of Hippo), to reevangelize Britain. After arriving, Augustine wrote to Gregory for advice on various issues he had encountered. One issue had to do with forms of worship. Having spent his whole life in Rome, Augustine had only known Christian worship as it was practiced in Rome. But in his travels he saw different customs and practices. When he came to evangelize the Britons he had the insight to wonder how to guide them in shaping their worship practices. Should he instruct them to copy Rome? Should he adopt practices he saw on the way from Rome to Britain? Gregory's reply was a model of wisdom and pastoral sensitivity:

Your brotherhood is familiar with the usage of the Roman Church, since you have very pleasant memories of being raised and nurtured in that usage.

But it seems to me that you should carefully select for the English Church—which is still new to the faith and developing as a distinct community—whatever can best please Almighty God, whether you discover it in the Roman Church, or among the Gauls, or anywhere else.

For customs are not to be revered for their place of origin; rather those places are to be respected for the good customs they produce.

From each individual church therefore, choose whatever is holy, whatever is awe-inspiring, whatever is right; then arrange what you have collected as if in a little bouquet according to the English disposition and thus establish them as a custom. (tr. Marie Conn, in James White, *A Brief History of Christian Worship*, Nashville: Abingdon Press, 1993, p. 44)

In this reply, Gregory had two particular insights for worship. The first insight is that different people have different manners and customs, different dispositions. This would seem obvious but remains elusive far too often in so many worship settings. Even something as simple as sitting versus standing means different things in different cultures. Physical touch means very different things in different cultures—a friendly western slap on the back would be considered highly offensive in much of the world. In the funeral traditions of some cultures, white apparel is a sign of mourning, whereas in other cultures the color of mourning is most definitely black. Wearing street shoes into the home or into a place of worship is acceptable in some cultures but not in others. These are not matters of right or wrong, but simply of differing manners and customs. Gregory told Augustine to literally pick and choose whatever he could find that would best serve the nascent English church by fitting the manners and customs of its people.

Gregory's second insight was that worship needs an arrangement of good manners and customs to be sustainable. There is no worship life without a sustainable ritual life, and creating such a ritual life takes great thoughtfulness, insight, understanding, and care. It also takes intentionality: he instructs Augustine to quite deliberately create new customs.

Augustine went on to baptize the first Christian King of England (Æthelberht of Kent) and indeed to establish the worship of the English church according to its own customs. Centuries later, his work continued to bear fruit with the production of the first national service book in English, the 1549 *Book of Common Prayer* (*BCP*). To this day the *BCP* tradition continues to be the heart of English-language liturgical worship.

My own introduction to the study of worship came when I was preparing to get married. My then-fiancée and I liked the idea of traditional vows ("take this man...take this woman...," "to have and to hold from this day forward, for better, for worse...") and it occurred to me to wonder where those phrases had come from. They beautifully express a biblical standard for marriage as lifelong, unconditional, and exclusive. But they are not words from the Bible. I learned they are words from the *BCP*, almost as old as anything else we have in English, and part of a treasury of other forms for church and worship use. The *BCP* magnificently expresses the English disposition towards orderliness, reserve, ceremony, and propriety. Alongside the works of Shakespeare and the Authorized ("King James") Version of the Bible, the *BCP* is one of the early pillars of modern English. And this was in part because of Gregory's good advice to Augustine.

Gregory recognized the good and needful role of contextualization. He could have told Augustine to simply transplant the Roman approach to worship as the "right" or at least the "best" way. But Gregory understood that no single culture has a lock on the right way to worship as Christians, not even the culture of Rome. Every culture can and should use its own gifts to create ways and customs to cultivate its own expressions of Christian worship. If I might paraphrase Gregory's advice, here's how I would imagine him writing today about ANA worship settings:

> Your leaders are familiar with the usage of majority-culture churches, since you have some good memories of being raised and nurtured in that usage.
>
> But it seems to me that you should carefully select for the Asian North American Church—which in many ways is still new to the faith and developing as a distinct community—whatever can best please Almighty God, whether you discover it in the black church, or in Australia, or among the Episcopalians, or on YouTube, or in your people's homes and restaurants, or in their festivals, or at their campus ministries, or in their ancestral customs, or anywhere else.
>
> For customs are not to be revered for their peoples and places of origin; rather those peoples and places are to be respected for the good customs they produce.
>
> From all different peoples and places therefore, choose whatever is holy, whatever is awe-inspiring, whatever is right; then arrange what you have collected as if in a little bento according to the Asian North American disposition and thus establish them as a custom.

Not Your Country but the Faith

Over a millennium later, in 1659, and regarding worship halfway around the world, Pope Alexander VII gave these remarkable instructions regarding missionary activity in East and Southeast Asia:

> Do not in any way attempt, and do not on any pretext persuade these people to change their rites, habits and

customs, unless they are openly opposed to religion and good morals. For what could be more absurd than to bring France, Spain, Italy or any other European country over to China? It is not your country but the faith you must bring, that faith which does not reject or belittle the rites or customs of any nation as long as these rites are not evil, but rather desires that they be preserved in their integrity and fostered. It is, as it were, written in the nature of all men that the customs of their country and especially their country itself should be esteemed, loved and respected above anything else in the world. There is no greater cause of alienation and hatred than to change the customs of a nation...Admire and praise whatever merits praise. (*The Christian Faith in the Doctrinal Documents of the Catholic Church*, J. Neuner, SJ and J. Dupuis, SJ, eds., New York: Alba House, 1982, pp. 309–10)

What happened from there is a long and complex story, and unfortunately not one with a happy ending. (You can research the Chinese Rites Controversy to learn more.) But the wisdom, good sense, and simple respect of such instructions are both self-evident and surprising even today. How different would the history of Christianity in Asia be if missionaries from the western colonial powers had consistently taken this instruction to heart? And yet today, in our churches, is it clear that ANA identity and culture "should be esteemed, loved, and respected"? Have you and I made good and full efforts to "admire and praise whatever merits praise"? Are we making the same mistakes all over again, this time by ourselves?

Formal and Informal Context

I should note here that the "contextual" includes the "everyday" but is not limited to it. In life we all have everyday clothes and dress-up clothes, conversational speech and formal speech (for instance, forms for greeting elders on special occasions), everyday get-togethers and formal occasions (graduations, weddings, funerals), your mother's daily cooking and the occasional big restaurant splurge or party banquet, and so forth.

Christian worship is actually unusual in being a single setting in which both the formal and the informal have a proper place, side by side. Liturgical traditions have overtly formal speech alongside the more conversational speech of sermons, announcements, extemporaneous prayers, and so forth. Free worship traditions specialize in extemporaneous prayers and (nowadays) conversational-toned sermons, but also have plenty of ritualized speech (whether or not it is acknowledged as such and used well as such). And that is fine. To draw customs from a culture is thus to draw from both formal and informal parts of that culture.

This combination of the formal and informal in worship reflects a deeper theological reality: Christianity claims that God is both *transcendent* (found beyond the universe we inhabit and the finite categories and perceptions we are capable of) and *immanent* (found within the universe and what we can understand and perceive, including the most ordinary parts of everyday life). This is the profound mystery of the Incarnation, that an infinite God could somehow also become a finite human being, an infant even for a time. On one hand our worship settings cannot be other than immanent, for they exist in the universe we inhabit. However, aspects of our settings that point to realities beyond this universe can express the transcendent. And so there is room to express both in our worship: the sense of transcendence inspired by a soaring gothic cathedral and the accessible immanence of a nondescript warehouse worship space; the transcendence alluded to by enduring worship music from centuries ago and the immanence of the most recent styles and beats on the street; the transcendence suggested by the best of ancestral culture and the immanence of the latest minority-majority culture clash to make the news. Both immanence and transcendence express truths about God and so both sides belong in worship.

(For ANA settings, "embracing culture" automatically means "embracing cultures" (plural). ANA settings involve ancestral, immigrant, and native cultures; different regional and national roots; and a combination of minority and majority cultures, all in an unfolding mixture.)It is always complicated and full of tensions. (Right now, my [Chinese American] daughters are quite fully into "K-Pop," which is mostly music videos and drama series from South Korea.)

We can also add ANA's share of world culture, expressed in forms such as international pop music, film, and other media; the Olympics and other international sports movements; global social networking, Wikipedia, and other internet-based forms of borderless collaboration; global commerce and multinational corporations; and the huge cosmopolitan centers of many present and emerging megacities. All this shared world culture is also part of ANA culture. And whatever is in a particular ANA setting, that comprises the cultural context that can and must be embraced in worship.

Worship Is Counter-Cultural (Culture-Rejecting)

Some parts of each and every culture are frankly evil and need full condemnation and rejection. No matter what our racial, cultural, or national identity, we are all fallen by nature and by choice, individually and collectively, in our persons and in our institutions and systems.

In Chinese history, footbinding was a fully cruel and oppressive custom. It was practiced sometimes locally and sometimes widely for perhaps a millennium, ending in the twentieth century. (One of my grandmother's immigration papers included a checkbox to mark whether her feet were "bound" or "natural.") There is no adapting such a practice for good. In a Christian worldview that values the body as much as the soul, honors physical work as fully good and honorable, rejects intentional indolence and dependency, shuns ostentation, and values all people (absolutely including girls and women of all different social backgrounds) as equally valuable, there is no place for such a practice. When my own daughters were of the age when their (growing, happy, adorable) feet would have been bound in such times and places, it gave me horror and revulsion to think of it.

While God led the early church to embrace Gentile culture, there were of course aspects of that culture to be rejected. One thinks of Paul's admonitions to not live "like the Gentiles" especially in matters of sexual morality (e.g., 1 Thessalonians 4:5). One thinks of the cruelty of the Roman gladiatorial games. One thinks of the then-common practice of "exposing infants" (that is, leaving unwanted newborns in fields to die) and how the early Christians actually gained a reputation for rejecting that practice. These were all matters for counter-cultural response.

Of course, there are surely parts of our own cultures in the twenty-first century that are fully worthy of rejection as well. I think of our own patterns of family and community in western culture, such that homelessness is so widespread and intractable not just in urban centers but in rural and suburban neighborhoods across the country. What does that say about us as North American Christians? In a recent interview, the historian and author David McCullough was asked what our society might look back on someday with regret and puzzlement. "That we watched so much TV," was his reply. Does anyone today not agree that we would all do better to watch far less TV?

Yet some aspects of cultures need redemption and should not be simply discarded. Only parts of them need rejection.

For instance, many cultures have rituals around the time of death that, on one hand, simply honor the dead but, on the other hand, also do things most Christians would reject as being contrary to our faith. There is nothing unchristian about honoring the dead. Indeed, Christians as much as, if not more than, anyone should value each life as made in the image of God and as the object of God's care and sacrificial love. The Fifth Commandment to honor father and mother should surely not be taken just minimalistically (e.g., finish your vegetables when your parents tell you to) but more fully (i.e., honor your parents and the legacy of your ancestors at every stage in life). But Christians may rightly object to many non-Christian funeral practices. When it comes to rituals to ward off evil spirits, to invoke other gods, or to manipulate the spiritual realm in hopes of promoting good fortune, these are all contrary to the Christian calling of faith and trust in Christ. It behooves Christians to redeem the impulse to honor the dead, especially deceased relatives, and to create fully developed ways to do so in funerals and other remembrances.

Uproot It Imperceptibly

There are better and worse ways of being counter-cultural, especially if one comes as an outsider to a culture. The 1659 instruction from Pope Alexander VII cited above continues on this point with timeless wisdom and understanding:

> As regards what is not praiseworthy, while it must not be extolled…be prudent enough not to pass judgment on it…not to condemn it rashly or exaggeratedly. As for what is evil, it should be dismissed by a nod of the head or by silence rather than by words, without losing the occasions, when souls have become disposed to receive the truth, to uproot it imperceptibly.

This is just good common sense, pastoral sensitivity, and theological wisdom. No one wants to be told that things they once cherished and cared for should be abandoned, that they and their ancestors had been misguided and wrongheaded all along. No one wants to be shamed. (One could easily cite western individualism and materialism or ANA unlimited faith and trust in academic achievement or financial invulnerability.) Even when things that should be abandoned become ready to be abandoned, no one wants to be scolded and coerced into abandoning such things.

To believe we are all made in God's image is to believe that we have all been given the gift of moral will and agency. To believe we are all fallen is to believe none of us has the right to go about rashly condemning others. "Do not judge, so that you may not be judged" (Matthew 7:1). The best way to remove something that cannot be redeemed is to help people grow and learn so that they themselves choose to abandon or remove it. This is even good psychology: positive reinforcement works far better than negative reinforcement, especially in developing new behaviors. The best trainers and coaches mostly ignore unwanted behaviors as much as possible and reward wanted behaviors lavishly. The same principle works in work and home settings.

For example, ancestor rituals are deeply entrenched mostly because of the belief that deceased ancestors must be met and supplied with provisions for their afterlife journey, or else they can and will cause trouble for those still in this life. (Although often called "ancestor worship" it is thus more accurately described as "ancestor appeasement" or "ancestor veneration.") A Christian could come to a new convert's house and demand that the ancestral altar be removed (and destroyed! and burned!), declaring, "Choose you this day whom you will serve!" Or the Christian can patiently teach and model how God's love and power are greater than those of any other spirit; that the dead in fact have no power over the living; and that Jesus made it possible for us to live by grace and faith bringing peace, not by works and duties based in fear. The Christian can also make real efforts to find caring, grateful, attractive ways to honor ancestors, ways that the convert would not be embarrassed to share with family and friends. All this, over time, will lead the convert to change both the outward practice and the inward belief.

Christianity does ask for exclusive loyalty to Jesus, the worship of God alone, and dependence on the Holy Spirit alone for the power to live our lives. There is no room for trust in other gods, spirits, or powers. There is no room for astrology or divination. (I personally try to keep a pretty wide boundary on this. For instance, I actually could not even tell you what astrological signs my wife and children are.) There is no room for a materialistic trust of wealth or power. There is no "playing the field." However, in practice, there are many cases that may or may not be as clear-cut as they may first seem. Let me mention a few examples without trying to settle them one way or the other: ~no~

Eating at a restaurant with an active altar. You've seen these: a red or rosewood open cabinet with food offerings; incense; candles; auspicious sayings on bright paper; and statues of *Guan Yu* (beard, red face, pole sword), *Budai* (commonly known as the "Laughing Buddha" because of his big belly and jovial expression, but who is actually a deified monk and not the Buddha), one or more of the *Fu Lu Shou* live-long-and-prosper astral guys, or *Guanyin* (the Goddess of Mercy). Does such an altar effectively render the restaurant an idol temple, and therefore a place to be shunned (1 Corinthians 10:14)? What about the presence of symbols of good luck or prosperity, such as a Japanese *Maneki Neko* "Lucky Cat" waving in prosperity, or a Thai/Laotian image of the female spirit *Nang Kwak*? What about other objects to attract good fortune or apotropaic objects to repel bad fortune (e.g., an eight-sided *bagua* mirror with Taoist symbols, meant to deflect "bad" *qi* energy)?

Wearing a "spirit string" blessed by a monk and meant to ward off evil spirits. Should a (new) believer remove and perhaps destroy such an object, perhaps on the example of the Ephesian sorcerers who burned their scrolls (Acts 19:19)? On one hand, there are any number of anecdotes about objects seemingly possessed by demons or providing an entrée for demonic powers. On the other hand, Paul could say that a physical idol itself is not anything, and that only actual acts of worship and devotion involved participation with demons (1 Corinthians 10:19-20; *cf.* 8:4, Deuteronomy 4:28, Psalm 115:4-5, Isaiah 41:21-24; 44:12-20; but possibly contrariwise are the demon-possessed swine of Mark 5:13). Is it then only a matter of associations? "Since some have become so accustomed to idols until now, they still think of the food they eat as food offered to an idol; and their conscience, being weak, is defiled" (1 Corinthians 8:7). Is the association with an unchristian source then the only difference between the use of an amulet and the use of a Christian object such as wearing a cross? Or is it ultimately simply a matter of the differing beliefs and faith commitments attached to a given object? (What if a new string were dedicated to Christ alone? How would that compare to the use of, say, wedding rings in Christian marriages?)

Using feng shui design elements. Water features and curved paths and furniture arranged in significant directions are all part of feng shui. At what point are such things an actual attempt to manipulate *qi* (life energy) and at what point are they simply an aesthetic tradition? Is this another area in which only intentions matter (Do I believe my windows need to face a certain way for my life to be blessed?) and actual objects or arrangements have no inherent power? Of course, given human nature, matters of belief and intention are never cut and dry, so it is never a clear case.

Using symbolically significant decorations and objects from nature. Lotus flowers on a banner, citrus fruit stacked for good health—these are cherished symbols and common decorations in various Asian cultures. The water lotus is closely associated with Buddhism (the Buddha sits on the Lotus Throne) but not with Buddhist prayer or worship. Might it be a usable symbol of Christian purity or water baptism? Oranges and tangerines are traditionally stacked as a symbol of physical life and health, but would it ever be appropriate to use them to decorate a

Communion table (perhaps during the Lunar New Year) to symbolize new life and hope through Jesus' body and blood? If people themselves can be redeemed and rededicated, cannot objects and forms?) Hmm..

Using symbols such as an Asian dragon on objects in a worship setting. Would you serve Communion on a platter decorated with a dragon motif? On one hand the Asian dragon is a mythical creature associated with blessing and prosperity. It is benevolent and generally not an object of worship. It symbolizes authority, justice, strength, and blessing—all qualities Christians would readily attribute to Christ. On the other hand, the dragon resembles the sea monster of the Ancient Near East that opposes God (Psalm 74:13), and ultimately the dragon of Revelation 12 and Satan as "that ancient serpent" of Revelation 20. But are the Asian and biblical dragons actually two different creatures, combined accidentally by a superficial resemblance and a shared English name? I have never known a Christian to shun as satanic all the restaurants with dragon names or decor, parade dragons at Lunar New Year celebrations, or designs such as the current dragon-themed civic promotional symbol for Hong Kong. (Might we need to do more sorting out here?) Is there room in Christian worship for extra-biblical mythical beings that convey biblical truths? (Note that there are numerous passages in Scripture that use clearly mythical Ancient Near Eastern creatures to depict God's work, e.g., the multi-headed Leviathan in Psalm 74:13-14.)

Praying and worshipping with forms and objects associated with other religions. Are we free to use incense sticks, certain postures for meditation (perhaps the lotus position, with legs crossed on thighs), chimes or bells to frame prayers, musical genres used in non-Christian worship, or foods with non-Christian symbolic meanings? It seems to me these are objects and forms that are neutral in and of themselves, though they may be associated with non-Christian spirituality and worship. Again, it would seem the

objects and forms are an issue only when they trouble the conscience of someone who cannot disassociate them from the worship of other spirits and gods. Indeed, if the body is God-given
and everything in creation is God-given, it's hard to think of a
prayer posture, or use of light or sound, or any particular natural object that could inherently not be used in Christian worship.
"The earth is the Lord's, and everything in it." (1 Corinthians
10:26, quoting Psalm 24:1, NIV). But that is different than saying
there is not wisdom and sensitivity in using or not using a particular form in a particular time and place, just as the Jerusalem
Council renewed the prohibition on eating blood (apparently to
avoid unnecessary offense, not because it was inherently sinful).

**Going through the motions of non-Christian rituals for the
sake of family peace, while inwardly praying and worshipping as
a Christian.** This is the situation of "Secret Christians." Some find
themselves in vulnerable and even life-threatening situations (a
minor, a dependent woman, a target of potential grave persecution) or situations of true responsibility (caring for needy relatives
and being unwilling to be shunned and have to leave them), and
so choose to keep their Christian faith covert. In this case, their
counter-cultural moves are inward and private. While such believers could "be like Daniel" and indeed openly risk everything, I
myself only feel admiration and compassion for anyone in such a
difficult and isolating situation (at least Daniel had his friends).

Of course I could have just as easily used counter-cultural
examples from western culture (its consumerism, individualism,
materialism, and so forth). However, I have focused on eastern
cultural forms because western forms in worship already dominate ANA churches. Surely it is worth pressing past superficial
objections ("that reminds me of what my grandparents did at the
temple") and freshly evaluating the full range of our bicultural
heritages for worship possibilities. (Besides, you could probably
find someone who would be reminded of this or that sub-
Christian setting by each of our various majority-culture worship

forms, e.g., the current prevalence of our use of stage-focused, highly produced worship music forms.)

Worship Is Cross-Cultural (Culture-Mixing)

Full and healthy worshipping communities build bridges between the cultures of their own members as well as bridges to their surrounding communities and the world at large. Especially in settings like so much of North America—where many peoples and cultures are to be found side by side, down the street, next door, and even within families—how can we not invite and celebrate a sharing of our various cultures as a shared offering to God?

That the great majority of ANAs live in spectacularly cosmopolitan cities and their surrounds (Toronto! New York! Los Angeles! the San Francisco Bay Area!) makes the need to share and mix all the more available and needful. In the small shopping district near my house, in a quite mixed-race part of Oakland, California, you can go out to eat at your choice of two Mexican restaurants, a McDonald's, a Japanese sushi restaurant, a local burger place, two pizza places, a Southern gumbo place, an Asian Indian restaurant, and fully five different Chinese restaurants (Full Moon, Asia House, Ly Luck, Flower Garden, and China Gourmet). And each and every one of those establishments would be most happy to serve you regardless of your own race, culture, or ancestry. Eating out in my neighborhood is a fully cross-cultural opportunity.

So it is when we share and borrow from each other's cultures in worship. But this is all the more reason to specially cultivate an ANA voice in worship—so as to have something to share in cross-cultural encounters. To take the restaurant metaphor further: for the most part, the ANA church has yet to create the menu, the manners, the ambience, the sensibilities, and the attractions that would be known and recognizable as ANA worship, to be appealing and desirable as ANA worship. This is the work we must do for the sake of the ANA church itself as well as for the sake of the wider church, which is not complete without the gifts of each and every "tribe and language and people and nation" (Revelation 5:9).

However, encounters between peoples and cultures is one of the great and enduring sources of conflict in the human condition. Throughout history there has been endless suffering and sorrow justified with hateful senses of "we" versus "they, and "us" versus "them." What might be better senses of approaching the real differences between peoples and cultures? One model I have found helpful is from Milton J. Bennett, now at his Intercultural Development Research Institute in Portland, Oregon. He proposes a six-stage developmental model of intercultural encounters:

Ethnocentric Stages

1. Denial. In *denial* we simply ignore differences and perhaps simply ignore other cultures, even ones that may be right next door to us. I think of so many churches in our cities, located within sight of each other or even on the same block and yet simply coexisting for years like ships passing in the night. We don't even talk to each other; we might as well be on different planets.

2. Defense. In *defense* we acknowledge other cultures but mostly to look down on them and feel superior to them. Perhaps we feel sorry for them but mostly we are glad we are not like *those people*. Sometimes this goes the other way as *reverse defense*: we feel inferior to others, and so envy them and perhaps try to imitate them. This reverse defense is not an objective view of differing cultural strengths (German efficiency, Italian style, English orderliness) but a deep-seated sense of cultural shame and inferiority. Sometimes this develops internally through self-sabotage (China's disastrous Great Leap Forward and Cultural Revolution) and other times through external devaluation (colonial powers treating local cultures as inferior, primitive, depraved, or repulsive). Whether in _defense_ or _reverse defense_ the defining characteristic is that different = bad.

3. Minimization. In _minimization_ we have acknowledged differences but we downplay the need to do much of anything about them. We are not motivated to change anything, especially our own inner attitudes about what we know of ourselves and others. This stage is often camouflaged with discussion-ending slogans such as, "There's only one race: the human race!" In churches this is a special hazard when there is a majority culture and one or more minority cultures. The mere presence of minority culture individuals is seen as a sufficient demonstration of accepting difference. There is no actual and sustained effort to incorporate the actual cultures of the minority members. This is also manifest when majority culture Christians express an interest in reaching out to minority cultures, meaning bringing "them" into "our" church. (If they really feel called to such outreach, maybe they should _find a minority culture church and join it and support it!_ Do they really care about those other people or not?)

These first three stages are ethnocentric in that they all keep one or the other culture in the center as the norm, standard, and model. If those involved have managed to get both cultures off that center, they are ready for the three ethnorelative stages.

Ethnorelative Stages

4. Acceptance. The first ethnorelative stage is _acceptance_, where "different = good" begins to be a possibility. Judgmental attitudes are defused and set aside. Both cultures are treated as admirable but also subject to fair-minded critique by self and others. There is enough of a spirit of trust to treat each other as cultural peers. (You will read more about such an encounter in Chapter 6 and the section on the "Crossings" black-Asian worship conference.)

5. Adaptation. In _adaptation_ we actually start to make space in our own settings for forms and values from the other culture.

We have pulpit and choir exchanges. We give other forms of prayer a try, perhaps a new experience of Korean *tongsungkido* unison spoken (shouted!) prayer, or black call-and-response prayer. We cultivate actual relationships with leaders across cultural boundaries (including, perhaps, those from other generations in our very own churches). We find occasions to tell stories and share insights from other cultures in admiring fashion. We truly see our own culture as one of many, each worthy of attention and respect.

6. Integration. Finally, in *integration* we actually let those other cultures shape and change us, and we are bold to share enough of ourselves that those other cultures want to be shaped and changed by us. The goal is not homogenization but mutual enrichment, with each culture becoming more fully and more beautifully itself the more it is shared. One of the particular reasons I greatly admire the black Baptist church is that it has well learned how to bring the pains and sorrows of its people into the worship moment (what are spirituals if not expressions of hope in the midst of suffering?). It seems to me that this is a particular weakness in ANA worship: we surely have our share of pains and sorrows but few ways to bring them to church. I want ANA worship to integrate into itself that aspect of Christian faith in black worship, a faith that believes there is room for such pain in worship, that such pain can and should be part of our self-offering on Sunday morning, and that we will meet and respond to God more fully, deeply, and joyfully by doing so.

If I can hazard a generalization, I would say much of the ANA church is (still, stuck—mostly unawares) in the *reverse defense* stage, basically treating the majority culture as better than ANA culture. We convey that the majority culture is Christian culture, and therefore majority-culture Christianity is essential to covey what saves. (In Chapter 7 I will press this point using the test case of what food and drink to set on the Lord's Table.) We are pretty early in the process of intercultural development. This is why it worries me when ANA church leaders seem anxious to "just be multicultural" without first paying good and full attention to cultivating ANA culture. It is also why I think there is very much a place for ANA churches and worship settings (even though they need to be vigilant about being more than a mere ethnic enclave). We still have some growing up to do before being able to fully engage the ethnorelative stages of *acceptance*, *adaptation*, and *integration*.

Niebuhr goes to Nairobi

Now with the four Nairobi categories in mind—transcultural, contextual, counter-cultural, and cross-cultural—you can see how unhelpful it is to get stuck on any one category. We can attempt a brief correlation with western theologian H. Richard Niebuhr's widely known five-way taxonomy from his 1951 classic book, *Christ and Culture*. We can approximate thusly:

1. *Christ of culture* (Christ to be found in the best of culture)
　　Nairobi *contextual:* Worship embraces the best of my culture.
　　Nairobi *cross-cultural:* Worship embraces the best of all others' cultures.
2. *Christ against culture* (culture is fallen, evil, and under judgment)
　　Nairobi *counter-cultural:* Worship stands in opposition and contrast to all that is contrary to God's commands and values, and to all that competes with exclusive loyalty to Jesus.
3. *Christ above culture* (culture is good but not sufficient)
　　Nairobi *contextual:* Worship embraces all the good in culture.
　　Nairobi *transcultural:* Worship includes all the ways Christ is present above and beyond every culture.
4. *Christ and culture in paradox* (culture is mixed and fallen, but still necessary and used by Christ)
　　Nairobi *counter-cultural:* Worship names and does not ignore or excuse what is fallen in culture.

Nairobi *contextual:* Worship embraces my culture even though it is ever a mixed bag of good and evil.

Nairobi *cross-cultural:* Worship embraces others' cultures even though each is ever a mixed bag of good and evil.

5. *Christ, transformer of culture* (culture is mixed and fallen and is being transformed by Christ)

Nairobi *transcultural, contextual, counter-cultural,* and *cross-cultural:* As worship appropriately relates to culture in all four categories, it brings about new life and growth.

To Niebuhr's five categories, I also add a sixth, "*Christ, sold out to culture*" (culture is sinful and fallen, but Christians chose to embrace it anyway, resulting in disobedience and hypocrisy). As has often been observed, the greatest barrier to the spread of the gospel is the lives of Christians who claim the name of Jesus but go on living as if their own comfort and security are what matter most. This too needs to be challenged in worship, in counter-cultural fashion.

I am making the argument throughout this book that Scripture does not give us any choice about engaging culture as we shape and order our worship lives. Hopefully these Nairobi categories can aid ANA worship leaders in that engagement, helping navigate past stuck points ("ANA culture is all good!" "ANA culture is all bad!") and prompting increasingly helpful discussions and explorations. Hopefully these categories can also help us approach the differing subcultures of our immigrant and later generations with helpful precision, insight, and expectations (e.g., expecting to find both good and bad beliefs and practices in both immigrant and Canadian/American-born generations). I pray that these Nairobi categories can also help us make a better, more balanced use of majority-culture forms, so that no one will have reason to think that "western" and "Christian" are one and the same.

It would be so much easier if God had simply given us a single, fixed form of worship. In faith we choose to believe that God truly enjoys the creative variety of all different forms for worship. We also choose to believe that as we give ourselves to this work, we will grow in our own character and in our capacity for truth, beauty, and joy. We are commanded, challenged, and reassured to "work out [our] own salvation with fear and trembling; for it is God who is at work in [us], enabling [us] both to will and to work for his good pleasure" (Philippians 2:12-13). Surely this (hard!) work of shaping and ordering our worship lives is no small part of that calling.

CHAPTER 5

Some Challenges

Why does the ANA church seem not very far along, and maybe even delayed, in the journey of finding its own voice and vision in worship? If worship and culture are so important, why do we seem to not be making an A+ effort to develop them together? (Do we even know there is an assignment, let alone knowing the questions on the assignment, let alone knowing how to go about working out the answers?) Let me suggest some possible reasons for this state of affairs, without trying to rank or weigh each of them.

A Still-Early History

The oldest Chinese church in America is San Francisco's Presbyterian Church in Chinatown, founded in 1853 and thus just a little more than a century and a half old. Compare this to the two oldest African American national denominations: the African Methodist Episcopal movement, founded in 1787 in Philadelphia, and the African Methodist Episcopal Zion movement, founded in 1796 in New York City. Thus, when the first Chinese church in America was just getting started (with mostly Caucasian leadership then and for decades following), the African American church already had two national denominations more than a half-century old. By historical standards, the ANA church is young.

The first American-born Chinese pastor to make his career in the United States was Edwar Lee (1902–96), who for many years was pastor of Oakland's Chinese Community United Methodist Church. He was ordained in 1936—still within living memory. In Atlanta, Georgia, in that same year, the Ebenezer Baptist Church celebrated its Golden Anniversary under the leadership of its third pastor, the Reverend Martin Luther King Sr. Thus, even the oldest groups within the ANA church are relatively young. No wonder we are, as a whole, just getting started on our journey of exploring and integrating matters of culture and identity into our worship.

Many other groups are far younger still. For instance, Southeast Asian immigration has taken place in large numbers going back barely two generations. Their first generation of leaders born or raised in North America are just now coming into full leadership roles. The first-ever national-level Southeast Asian Leadership Summit (SEALS) for Christian leaders took place in 2006 in Long Beach, California. The ANA church is young by historical standards.

Meanwhile, ANA culture in general is also young and still being formed. Even with enough titles now for annual Asian Canadian and Asian American film festivals and with college courses in Asian Canadian and Asian American literature, ANA culture at large is itself emergent, latent, and delitescent. In the realm of popular culture, we have still not found a way to sustain even one pan-Asian, general-interest, coast-to-coast ANA magazine. *A. Magazine* ran for 13 years and never made a dime before finally closing up shop in 2002, despite a large circulation and heavy funding. *Hyphen* is currently making a go at it, but with a volunteer-run, nonprofit model and a readership mostly consisting of the progressive young adult ANA market. *AsianWeek* has been in publication since 1979 but continues to search for a consistent editorial focus and evenness of more than local (i.e., Bay Area) coverage. And in 2009 *AsianWeek* stopped its print edition (although that was partly a reflection of industry-wide trends). We can be thankful for all such media efforts, but their struggles are a symptom of the still-young state of ANA culture and identity.

Scattered Stories

ANA immigration has been scattered, occurring over many different times and under many different circumstances. There is no one central narrative (such as slavery and then the civil rights movement for African Americans, or genocidal dispossession of the land for Native Americans) to help shape the sense of shared identity and journey as a people.

Where there is a living memory of shared suffering, the results have been striking. For instance, the internment camp experience of Japanese Americans during World War II led in no small part to the creation of the Japanese American National Museum in Los Angeles, a spectacular, world-class display of the Japanese American experience in general and the internment camp experience in particular. One might compare it to the equally important but far more modest Chinese American Museum of Los Angeles, beautifully and meaningfully located nearby in El Pueblo de Los Angeles Historic Monument, in the oldest surviving Chinese commercial building in Southern California. I have had occasions to take seminary classes to visit the two museums, walking from one to the other for back-to-back visits. The contrast in scale never fails to make a deep impression.

In truth, the story of historic anti-Chinese violence, discriminatory legislation, and racial prejudice in California and elsewhere remains to be widely told and acknowledged—perhaps there may yet be a fuller and more powerful telling. Many Southeast Asians of differing ancestries have shared immigration experiences involving the U.S. war in Vietnam, the Killing Fields in Cambodia, the refugee camps in Thailand and elsewhere, and involuntary resettlement in North America. Such shared experiences of suffering are leading to a shared remembering and telling of history. Still, these are separate, scattered stories, not (yet) coalesced into a fully shared ANA story.

Just knowing someone is of, say, Chinese ancestry tells you very little about their actual family background. How long ago did their family first immigrate and from where? Did they speak Cantonese, Mandarin, Taiwanese, Fukinese, a rural dialect, or something else? Were they peasants, merchants, students, entrepreneurs, civil servants, or academics? Were they already part of the Chinese diaspora, say, in Vietnam? Was there a Chinese presence where they settled in North America? Two different Chinese North Americans could very easily have less in common with each other than with non-Chinese ANAs of a more similar background.

Meanwhile, the stories get ever more mixed as increasing numbers of ANAs marry "out," whether to Asians of other ancestries (I recently went to a wedding where the bride's family is Chinese from Taiwan and the groom's family is Filipino from Guam) or to non-Asians. The stories are varied and getting more and more so.

Immigration Trends

First-generation immigrant culture continues to dominate the ANA communities with high immigration rates. The majority of ANA residents are first-generation, even after a century and a half of immigration. This is partly due to the U.S. Chinese Exclusion Act and subsequent legislation, which severely restricted immigration from 1882 to 1965; and to the Canadian Chinese Immigration Act and subsequent legislation, which did the same from 1885 to 1967. Were it not for those exclusions, there would be vastly more families now in their fourth and fifth generations, with much more shared history, accomplishments, and resources to add to the ANA story.

The net effect is that immigrant culture still dominates, leaving less "space" for a distinctive ANA culture to emerge. Indeed, some observe that immigrant culture sometimes becomes "fixed" in the cultural time point at which it migrated, so that some immigrant communities incorporate more features of their ancestral settings from times past than those ancestral settings currently do in the actual present. For instance, you might find more traditional Chinese wedding customs being practiced today in Vancouver than in Hong Kong.

Immigration Motivations, Social Position, and Assimilation

For the most part, ANA immigration has been voluntary, so these immigrants have been generally inclined to assimilate within a generation or so. To adopt majority-culture forms and ways of expression has been deemed generally unobjectionable and even aspirational. Furthermore, since the majority culture in North America is majority-Christian, the majority culture also defines the cultural sense of Christianity here, including what is considered culturally normal in worship. ANA worship settings are caught between assimilating to the majority culture on the one hand and being perceived as foreign on the other.

To make things worse, the social position of ANA citizens and residents remains surprisingly tenuous. As recently as 2003, the late Iris Chang could end her book, *The Chinese in America: A Narrative History* (New York: Penguin) with a final chapter titled "An Uncertain Future." Just in early 2011 there were two media incidents that highlighted the ongoing debate over Asian presence and culture: the debate over Amy Chua's *Battle Hymn of the Tiger Mother* (New York: Penguin) and the reaction to the "Asians in the Library Rant" video made by former University of California, Los Angeles student Alexandra Wallace. (Chua's book was taken by many as a Chinese critique of western parenting standards; Wallace's video was a blunt complaint about the threat she perceived from Asian students' "otherness" in manners, languages, and family roles.) While both tempests have, it would seem, led to worthwhile dialog and reflection, that they happened at all is evidence of "unassimilation." To experience this still-tenuous social position is to experience pressure to assimilate to the majority culture.

Missions History

The overwhelming share of ANA Christianity traces its roots back to western missionary and evangelism efforts both in North America and in Asia. I myself am fully thankful that the Christian beliefs of my grandparents, my parents, I myself, and now my own children are all among the countless fruits of western Christianity on these shores. Would that my own life might someday leave a legacy of anything like such evangelistic commitment, sacrifice, effort, and care.

At the same time it is fair to say that such missionary and evangelism efforts conflated "western" and "Christian" more often than not. Indeed, damage in particular from the pairing of western colonialism with western missions remains to this day, with Christianity still widely considered foreign and western. While watching the 2008 Beijing Olympics and being overwhelmed by the enormous effort that went into hosting them, one of my prayers was that, when all was said and done, China could put to rest at least a little more the colonial ghosts of the past and the ways in which those ghosts still color the identity and reputation of Christianity in China.

Historically, there have certainly been western missionaries who made significant efforts at cultural contextualization. In China, Matteo Ricci (1552–1610) mastered classical Chinese and embraced Confucian categories of thought in how he communicated the Christian faith. In India, Roberto de Nobili (1577–1656) became the first foreigner to master Sanskrit and

Tamil, to become an expert in the Hindu sacred texts, and to learn to fully navigate the complex local social system. In Burma, Adoniram Judson (1788–1850) built a *zayat*—a Burmese-style roadside public meeting house—and there taught from the first Burmese Bible, which he himself translated. In China, Hudson Taylor (1832–1905) made it a point to dress and wear his hair as an indigenous Chinese and required his coworkers to do the same. And all these men persisted in such efforts despite sometimes heavy and even escalating criticism by colleagues and superiors, sometimes to the highest levels of their ecclesiastical hierarchies.

Meanwhile, home missions to immigrant communities in North America have also overwhelmingly privileged western forms of worship, evangelism, and spirituality. I myself grew up with the 1972 bilingual Chinese-English hymnal *Hymnody,* compiled and translated in Berkeley by Moses Lee Kung Yu. Of the nearly 600 texts and tunes, all but a handful are translated western hymns and gospel songs. Of course, there is no reason ANA believers cannot make their own claim to that western repertoire as part of their own heritage. But imagine the story turned around: what if Europe had been evangelized by Asian missionaries who insisted on establishing and perpetuating a transplanted Asian expression of Christian faith and worship, and then transplanted those Asian forms onto the first churches in North America? Would anyone think that was a good idea? Yet that is exactly the kind of transplanting and cultural imposition that the ANA church has inherited.

East versus West

Let me highlight two particular dynamics of east versus west culture clashes and how they have delayed the development of ANA worship.

Reservation versus Self-Expression

First, insofar as eastern culture is more reserved, deferential, and focused on group harmony, it is at odds with western and especially U.S. culture's values around self-expression, individualism, and extroversion. True, everyone who wants to share in the common life in North America needs to somehow embrace the freedom of speech that is the basis of so much of both our political systems and our wider social fabric. In order to get along we depend on each other to speak up. Even those of us from more reserved ancestries and cultures need to adapt at least in part to the more expressive shared culture on these shores.

Nevertheless, the clash is real and efforts to embrace and express more-reserved cultural ways will feel as if they are going against the grain. I find myself concerned with the full embrace of western praise music in so many ANA churches, if only because that particular musical genre seems to work best for more extroverted, more openly expressive personalities and cultures (befitting its origins in western culture). It coveys that "good worshippers" are the ones who embrace what is simply one cultural form.

Confucian Duty versus Christian Redemption

Second, the Confucian sense of duty does not provide a ready entrée to a public posture of neediness, especially in a typical church setting that includes many outside of one's family and many strangers. The Confucian ideal is to quietly tend to one's family responsibilities at whatever cost necessary, without asking for pity or for help. In contrast, the Christian gospel proclaims there is grace, forgiveness, and redemption even when we (inevitably) fall short, whether in our outward duties or our inward motivations. But to proclaim this good news and to express it in worship is to admit that we are sinners who need saving, and that we cannot save ourselves. This is a tall order in a shame-based culture. We are raised our whole lives to focus on duty, responsibility, and obligation. We are taught to "save face" at all costs. (Even when perhaps ready to share vulnerably and in repentance, how often do we nevertheless find ourselves determined to do so in just the right and best way—that is, as yet another exercise in dutiful achievement and self-justification?) There must be culturally appropriate ways to challenge the supposed need to save face without unnecessary confrontation and shame. Some groups have developed gospel presentations that are more about biblical images of being adopted into God's family, or returning to the Father, or other more Asian-friendly depictions, and not the individualistic or confrontational approaches more common in western presentations of the gospel. But there is a fundamental challenge in proclaiming a message of forgiveness and redemption in a culture focused on duty and shame.

Fears of Syncretism

Worship forms that feel "eastern" may evoke fears of syncretism, since both historically and presently the most visible religions in East and Southeast Asia are Buddhism and Taoism. (Recall however that Buddhism itself came to the Far East as a missionary religion, with its roots in South Asia.) Just a mention of meditation or the use of chimes, incense, or chanting may feel too close to the worship practices of these other religions to be used in Christian worship and spirituality.

Indeed, perhaps this provides some additional motivation for ANA churches to readily assimilate to majority culture worship forms, since the generational movement from immigrant ancestral culture to western culture has accompanied a movement from Buddhism and Taoism to Christianity. Temples and monks are what our families left behind. Some traces crossed with them and are lingering here, but they feel like part of the past, not the future. So ANA churches largely do not aspire to what feel like backward-looking, spiritually abandoned forms.

But there are also forms and objects that are not inherently syncretistic, even though they may sometimes be associated with rival faiths. I grew up in a Baptist church that did not use candles or incense in worship. Down the street was a Buddhist temple that very prominently featured candles and incense. Is there anything inherently Buddhist about candles or incense? Of course not: not any more than having a building dedicated to worship, or lights, or recognized leaders, or prayers, or money offerings, or religious music, or any number of other shared religious forms. Are Baptists free to use candles and incense in worship? Absolutely—but within the bounds of love regarding any actual matters of conscience (not just matters of preference or taste).

Meanwhile, it is not as if western Christianity is somehow free from syncretism with rival faiths and secular forms. Our very English word "God" most likely had its origins in Proto-Germanic words with Proto-Indo-European roots involving terms for prayer or worship, all very pre-Christian. We make do with the use of a capital "G" but this is a modern, western adaptation (the use of majuscule and minuscule letters for what we know today as mixed-case typography did not begin until the time of Charlemagne [742–814]). The common biblical terms for God (Hebrew 'ēl and Greek *theos*) were also generic and widely used for other deities. Our very days of the week and months of the year—printed right there in our church bulletins—include numerous pagan deities (e.g., "January" from the Roman god Janus, "Wednesday" from the Germanic/Anglo-Saxon god Woden). "Easter" derives from the Anglo-Saxon goddess Eostre. Our large church buildings are usually patterned after Roman basilicas or modern theaters or concert halls. Choir robes and preaching robes originated in medieval universities. Office titles like "senior pastor" are more from corporate business use than from Scripture (where "pastor" is a gift, not an office). On-screen song lyrics came from the world of entertainment. And on and on it goes; it's hard to find any form that does not have a mixed pedigree.

At the same time, there may well be things we can learn from and admire from rival faiths, for instance, Buddhist attention to meditation as a prayer form and Islam's group discipline in public prayer. Christianity can and must follow its inherently centrifugal cultural trajectory, and this will always involve tensions with matters of conscience and risks of syncretism. Is there anything in ANA ancestral culture that is not, to some degree, Buddhist/Taoist/Confucian (with the notable special case of the Philippines and its very long history with Roman Catholicism)? That doesn't mean ancestral culture is to be abandoned wholesale, any more than western culture is to be shunned wholesale for being thoroughly materialistic and individualistic. All cultures are to be embraced with care and discernment, fully aware of actual risks of syncretism but generously avoiding guilt by mere association.

Theological Tilt

All acknowledge that the ANA church is overwhelmingly populated by evangelical and otherwise more conservative theological identities, leaders, and associations. As a self-identified evangelical myself, I both invest myself in and truly wish the best for ANA evangelicalism—and I am also acutely aware of its particular weaknesses. Among those weaknesses is a free-worship biblicism that has too rarely thought through why it does what it does on Sunday mornings. We assume that our worship practices are simply and happily in obedience to Scripture. We might not see the point of fully engaging matters of history, tradition, or cultures, even while being shaped by them in multitudes of ways. I believe that evangelical commitments to the authority of Scripture are good and worthwhile, and I have devoted a great deal of my life, education, and ministry to such commitments.

But perhaps I can therefore be allowed to point out this unhelpful side effect of such commitments, that they have not prompted needed attention to matters of culture and identity that I believe are vital if ANA worship is to flourish.

Even worse, I think there are times when free church evangelicals see historic Christian worship customs (e.g., liturgy) and dismiss them as something done by our theological opposites, whether Catholics or mainline Protestants. Worship forms become an unwitting and unfortunate pawn in a social sense of "we" versus "they." We don't cross ourselves because that's what Catholics do, even though that Christian ritual gesture is far more ancient than what we call Roman Catholicism. We don't genuflect or kneel or bow. We don't walk in procession or light candles or preside in robes or use a service book (except maybe at weddings). Pretty soon we aren't doing much of anything at all.

Free church evangelicals stake much on our conservatism regarding historic, orthodox doctrines such as Jesus' full divinity and the final authority of Scripture. The irony is that when it comes to worship forms, *we are the "liberals"!* We look down on those whose theology might come from casual, passing fashions and popular opinion, but that is *exactly* how many of us shape our worship forms. Further, we claim to be led in worship moment by moment by the Holy Spirit—but does that mean we ignore what the Holy Spirit led the church to create and experience over the past twenty centuries? (Eastern Orthodox worship takes the exact opposite approach. There the assumption is: if the Spirit led the church to true and beautiful forms centuries ago, why change them now?)

Conservatives may reflexively hesitate to be culturally creative in worship forms because some kinds of creativity and change may feel "liberal." Yes, we can change the music, and yes, we can change the seating arrangement. But change the purple grape juice and somehow it feels like going down a slippery slope that could lead to tampering with our belief in Jesus' bodily resurrection.

Continuity in ritual forms is not a small thing at all, nor is the role of ritual forms in constructing identity and community. But using purple grape juice is already a culturally creative, scripturally very "liberal" practice. (I will explore the history of the use of purple grape juice for Communion in Chapter 7.) As such, I don't think it has the theological credentials for anything like an authoritative, unchanging form.

So, to the degree that the ANA church is dominated by evangelical and conservative believers, there is extra work to be done in adjusting our sensibilities and theological approach around matters of worship.

Underinvestment in Leadership

I am thankful that my own parents always wholeheartedly encouraged me to go into the ministry, and that my in-laws (who were not believers when my wife and I married) did not raise any objections to my education and career choices. Nevertheless, in the ANA community at large, the Christian ministry is not anywhere near the top of the list of widely approved and encouraged career choices. Here in California there is sometimes the unspoken sense that ministry is for nice guys (and, occasionally, gals) who "couldn't make it in the *real* world." I am being blunt. But there is no question that our best and brightest ANAs are far more likely to go to medical school, law school, business school, or a graduate engineering program than to go to seminary. Those are all good and worthy callings. But there is a price to be paid if we do not in costly fashion invest in the leadership of our worship settings.

In the mid-twentieth century, the majority of Christian worship traditions worldwide participated to one degree or another in what became known as the Liturgical Renewal Movement. It was a huge investment in historical and biblical scholarship, theological reflection, and publication of new liturgies and instructions for worship. For Roman Catholics, it culminated in the work of Vatican II, which ended four centuries of almost static worship forms in Latin. For the participating Protestant traditions, it resulted in a whole new generation of primary service books. The movement came to a consensus about the norm of weekly worship being a service of Word and Table (with Catholics generally needing to shore up the place of the Word in its worship, and Protestants generally needing to do the same for the Table). The movement produced a complete three-year lectionary of Scripture selections for daily and weekly worship, carefully structured around the four Gospels and the church year, and setting out four Scripture readings for use each Sunday. Furthermore, the movement articulated shared affirmations and points of disagreement about matters such as baptism.

Free church evangelicals pretty much sat out and ignored this entire effort, from beginning to end. Part of the reason was because of theological and institutional distancing from the participating groups. But another part was because we simply did not have scholars and leaders with expertise in such things, nor institutions of our own to train them even if we had felt a need to do so (for many years there have been no seminary-based doctoral programs in liturgical studies at evangelical institutions).

Surely something is wrong when parts of the ANA community can be so notably high-achieving in many other endeavors (academics, professions) and yet so notably low-achieving in theological leadership. Doesn't our worship life deserve as full an investment of our abilities as all the other things we sacrifice so much for and work so hard to achieve?

Helpful but Challenging Senses of Authenticity

Three senses of authenticity are helpful but nevertheless create challenges for cultivating ANA worship. The first helpful sense of authenticity is an emphasis on frankness and honesty at church, acknowledging that we all come to church openly needy and that the church is fundamentally a spiritual *hospital* and not a spiritual *hall of fame*. Church should be a safe place for broken, needy people to come and not have to hide behind smiling faces. For the ANA church, this kind of authenticity is risky and challenging, breaking through the Confucian values and habits of shame-based face-saving. There are culturally different ways to express spiritual neediness, and the specific challenge for the ANA church is to find its own "voice" in expressing that neediness in worship.

The second helpful but challenging sense of authenticity is an invitation for ANA worshippers, who may have been raised to ignore and suppress their inner and especially emotional lives, to find emotional connection and healing in worship. While our emotional lives are not the center, goal, and measure of authentic worship, they are certainly part of who we are, and therefore part of our full self-offering in worship. One can hope that the ANA church will develop understanding and practices here that can enable full emotional engagement in worship in ways that are specially appropriate for ANA worshippers, that we will not covey that to be a good worshipper one must, say, "act white" or "act black." But imitation is easy; self-searching and creativity are much harder.

The third helpful but challenging sense of authenticity for ANA worshippers is the freedom to experience acts of worship as invitational rather than directive. In a culture that emphasizes the group over the individual, there is a need to specially give permission to not always have to sing when everyone else is singing, or say words of response ("Thanks be to God"), or put anything in the offering plate, or take Communion. God invites and does not force or coerce. In this sense, worship should be individually authentic, a willing offering. In recent years I am glad to generally see more freedom in this area in ANA churches. However, it will remain a special challenge to cultivate a helpfully ANA sense of individual choice when it comes to active participation in worship.

Unhelpful Senses of Authenticity

There are other senses of authenticity that are not helpful for ANA worship or anywhere else. Let me mention three. The first is the postmodern value placed on subjective, inward experience as being authentic beyond anything outward and objective. (Students of nineteenth-century European history will recognize the similarities with the *Sturm und Drang* movement and the development of European romanticism as a reaction to Enlightenment rationalism and to the Industrial Revolution.) Here, authenticity is ultimately a matter of inward individual experience, connected (if at all) to historical and physical reality only out of convenience. The ANA church and the church at large should rather strive for a balance between the objective and the subjective, the outward and the inward. This befits basic Christian claims about the nature of creation and of our identity as both physical and spiritual beings. A dependence on only the subjective is especially unhelpful for emergent expressions of worship such as in the ANA church, since sustainable worship traditions cannot be constructed from subjective individual experiences.

The second unhelpful sense of authenticity is an uncritical trust in our impulses and inclinations. (Unfortunately, these are the very same impulses and inclinations promoted by our consumeristic, media-driven culture.) If we believe in human fallenness, we should be wary of what we bring to church inside us. Depending on my sinful "just as I am" to shape and express my worship can certainly be hazardous. Sometimes this is obvious, as when worship becomes a place for ego displays, self-righteousness, or, conversely, self-hatred. Even apart from such negative motivations, we may simply be untrained and undisciplined in worship. I should not be surprised if worship asks me to do things that are unfamiliar or uncomfortable because worship is training me to do something my sinful self does not want to and does not know how to do. Worship is a spiritual discipline more than it is spiritual recreation. ANA worship, being young and in formation, specially needs building blocks that are more sound than individual impulses and inclinations.

Thirdly, authenticity is not helpful when it is used to mean, "You come up with some worship form out of yourself that therefore will be authentically yours." So many times I've heard leaders encourage worshippers to "worship any way you like: stand, sit, dance, however you want to express your worship." This can be good insofar as it counters inhibition borne of mere self-consciousness. But what we chiefly need is a full, usable, and sustainable vocabulary of gesture, movement, and actions in worship. Directing people in what to do can actually be more freeing and indeed more authentic than just leaving them to themselves. We don't encourage people to roll out of bed Sunday morning and come to church without grooming and changing from their pajamas. We (rightly) expect ourselves and others to adhere to cultural norms of appearance and dress. Such forms are hardly inauthentic; indeed, it is precisely in the variety and range of customary dress and grooming that we are able to express ourselves. In the same way, having shared and even conventional forms for worship are not antithetical to authenticity. It is actually just the opposite: only by having the forms and conventions of a shared worship life can we express ourselves to each other at all. Worship is a training ground and we should expect it to feel awkward, like someone learning how to dance. Dance instructors do not say, "Just move how you feel." It is only by (awkwardly) practicing directed movements that the student will, eventually, be able to dance, to be expressive in dance, and to feel the emotions of dancing. Thus, an open invitation to individualistic expression is not a useful shortcut to full and good worship forms. This is all the more true for ANA settings, where I believe we have a particular need for experimentation and the construction of new worship traditions. My hope is that it will lead to fresh experiences of authenticity beyond what people brought or could have generated on their own. Asking people to just do whatever they want will lead nowhere.

Platonic Residue

Recently I heard a thoroughly-churched preteen girl respond to the question, "What's the most valuable thing you have?" With admirable piety she replied, "My soul." What do you think of that reply? In Christian theology and thinking is the soul the most valuable thing we have? Is it more valuable than the body?

The idea of separating and elevating the immaterial parts of us above the material parts can be traced not to Scripture but rather mostly to Greek philosophy. For thinkers such as Plato, the immaterial was the realm of ideals, truth, and beauty. The material world was lower, the realm of the imperfect and the corruptible. The material world was valuable only insofar as it pointed us to the immaterial world, where alone perfection could be found.

In fully Christian thinking, the material is *not* below the immaterial. Jesus went through a lot of trouble to get a body—and he's keeping it, forever. This constitutes the two supreme miracles at the very center of Christianity: Jesus' incarnation and resurrection. He "emptied himself, taking the form of a slave, being born in human likeness" (Philippians 2:7), this through the miracle and drama of Mary's virginal conception. Of Jesus' bodily resurrection Paul declared, "If Christ has not been raised, your faith is futile and you are still in your sins" (1 Corinthians 15:17). Even post-ascension, there was and will be no "uncarnation" or "discarnation." In his present mediatorial work, Jesus retains his full humanity (1 Timothy 2:5). There will be an essential continuity between our present, mortal bodies and the glorified, supernatural bodies like Jesus' (he as the resurrection "first fruit" [1 Corinthians 15:20-23]) that we will have someday. The New Heaven and New Earth will be populated by embodied, active beings, not spirits on clouds. The resurrection of the body (not just the immortality of the soul) is one of the core beliefs in the ancient Christian creeds. In Christian thinking, the material world and we as embodied creatures are created by God and declared as good and very good. Sin has corrupted material creation and brought physical suffering and mortality to our existence but this is part of what God is redeeming. "We know that the whole creation has been groaning in labor pains until now; and not only the creation, but we ourselves, who have the first fruits of the Spirit, groan inwardly while we wait for adoption, the redemption of our bodies" (Romans 8:22-23). In the Christian view of things, being an embodied spirit is a profound matter with eternal prospects.

And to have a body is to inescapably interact with culture. You cannot have a body without looking a certain way in relation to others; eating and enjoying some foods more than others; having a particular mother tongue and heart language, relating to your family and friends in some ways and not others; having certain sensibilities about time; working thorough particular issues of identity; interacting with other people with a particular vocabulary of gestures, postures, and motions; and even simply having a name that locates you within a particular social place and era. To have a body is to be a cultural being.

But western culture is still heavily influenced by Platonic thinking, probably more than we realize. In so many of our churches, the worship experience is actually quite platonic, with lots of sitting quietly while idealized ideas (and now images) are broadcast. Churches that emphasize preaching can be especially prone to this. Hearing a sermon can be a fully embodied experience, but it can also, and perhaps more easily, be mostly a mental experience. Are we giving our bodies a full and good range of ways to express our worship? I think of black Baptist churches I visit and of their beautifully full and good sense of embodiment: the very movement and sense of gathering and greeting, the call and response in prayer and preaching, the energetic ways of singing; it is all nothing if it is not embodied.

What might fully embodied worship look like in ANA culture, where our sensibilities are quite different but we have very same bodies? For instance, might there be an embodied sense of stillness we can specially cultivate in prayer, a stillness that might be a welcome relief from our constant streams of talk and activity?

From the other side of the world there are also Buddhist beliefs about the body: that it is ultimately an illusion along with everything else in the material world, that its attachments and desires are the root of manifest suffering. It's hard to say how much this influences worship in ANA settings. Probably of more influence is the still-ambivalent sense of ANAs' physical bodies as they are visibly different from the majority culture, especially as featured in the media and public figures. This is changing, with growing numbers of ANA professional athletes, actors, political officials, business leaders, and other highly visible figures creating new space for the physical presence and appearance of ANAs.

There is a common misreading of Jesus' encounter with the Samaritan Woman that bears clarification here. In the course of their conversation, she broached the topic of proper worship venues: must one worship in Jerusalem and not at the longstanding rival Samaritan site on Mt. Gerizim? Jesus answered, "Woman, believe me, the hour is coming when you will worship the Father neither on this mountain nor in Jerusalem....God is spirit, and those who worship him must worship in spirit and truth" (John 4:21,24).

The misreading is to take Jesus' words as meaning, "The body now doesn't matter in worship; only the invisible, inner parts matter." Rather, he is answering her question: where does my body need to be to worship? (The religious debate between the Jews and Samaritans was fundamentally geographical: which of their two rival temples was the right place to worship, the one in Jerusalem or the one on Mount Gerizim? This debate actually continues to this day.) And Jesus' answer is: your body can be *anywhere*, as long as you are worshipping in spirit and truth.

With the coming of Jesus, worship would no longer be based at a temple, that is, at a single physical place where God's presence would be localized. In time, God's presence would be localized in every gathering of believers, each of their very bodies a "temple of the Holy Spirit" (1 Corinthians 6:19). The coming of Jesus ushered in an era not of disembodied worship but of universally localizable worship.

Likewise there is a misreading of the command in Romans 12:1-2 to offer our bodies as living sacrifices, "which is [our] spiritual worship." The word translated "spiritual" does not mean "in contrast to material, physical" worship. (Indeed, did Paul not just specify this worship as a bodily act?) He did not use the word *pneumatikos* (which elsewhere might better be translated "supernatural" rather than "spiritual" if "spiritual" is taken to mean "immaterial," e.g., in 1 Corinthians 15:44). Rather, in Romans 12:1 he used *logikos*, which is related to the meaningfulness, purposefulness, and rationality of the *logos* "way." So here, one's "worship on the way" is specifically embodied, which means such worship always involves matters of culture. Culture matters because the body matters.

I once had an opportunity to visit the Church of the Nativity in Bethlehem. There, in a grotto below the altar, is the very spot where Jesus is believed (with reasonable historical credibility) to have been born, marked with a large silver star set in a marble platform. I was with fellow seminary students, all Protestant evangelicals. As we stood there, various pilgrims passed through to pray, variously kneeling, crossing themselves, touching the star, and performing other clearly physical acts of worship. We, on the other hand, mostly didn't know what to do with ourselves, even though we surely believed the same things as these pilgrims about the site's history and importance. Our only physical act was . . . to take pictures. And if you analyzed our motives, I imagine we were not so different from the pilgrims: we wanted to interact with the physical setting in a way that was worthy of its importance and that would partake of that importance so as to benefit our own lives. But we were acting more like students of Plato (if not simply tourists and consumers), while those pilgrims were acting more like worshippers of Jesus. Which approach to worship is more like what we typically find in ANA churches?

A Final Reflection

It's okay to be early in a journey and even to be somewhat delayed. I mention these dynamics not to cast blame or to complain, but simply to try to understand why the ANA church is where it is in its worship on the way. My hope is that by naming and better understanding these challenges and obstacles, we might be better positioned to cultivate ANA worship. Our present state of affairs was not inevitable and it is not immutable. But we will need to make conscious choices and exert patient effort to change directions.

Meanwhile, we have so much to work with: we have churches, leaders, traditions, educations, positions of responsibility, gifted artists and musicians, financial resources, buildings, the beautiful range of Asian ancestries and the developing sense of shared ANA identity, the differing gifts and emphases of the Canadian and American senses of multiculturalism, and the religious and social freedom to do with it all what we will. May "early and somewhat delayed" quickly become a thing of the past, yet in the process lead us to deeper and truer places than we might have gone otherwise.

CHAPTER 6

Explorations

Let me now share from my own journey in recent years of explorations of these matters of worship and culture, focusing on a series of worship projects and conferences I've been part of. As with all journeys, there are planned goals, there are things that are expected along the way, and there are also many surprises. In many ways, after these explorations, I feel like I have more questions than answers. But hopefully they are better questions than when I started.

Waterwind

In spring 2003 at the American Baptist Seminary of the West in Berkeley, California, I worked with a team that led what we believe was the first Asian American worship conference. We called the conference "Waterwind" and gathered 140 participants from forty Asian American churches for a day of music, teaching, conversation, food, and fellowship.

We chose the conference name "Waterwind" as an implicitly, indirectly Asian name for the conference. It's a reversal of "wind-water" or *feng shui*, the mostly Chinese belief that the orientation of buildings, doorways, windows, and furniture, along with the placement of other environmental features, affects the flow of life energy, *qi*. It is not just an aesthetic tradition, but a belief in a vital need to manipulate aspects of life in order to experience goodness and blessing in life. While not entirely rejecting *feng shui* insofar as it is now also sometimes simply an aesthetic tradition (involving, for instance, curved paths and water features in gardens), we wanted to express the Christian calling to approach life not via manipulation but via faith in a loving God. So we reversed "wind-water" to "water-wind," echoing Jesus' words to Nicodemus in John 3:5, "Very truly, I tell you, no one can enter the kingdom of God without being born of water and Spirit [*pneuma,* "wind"]." We also thought a more implicit name that evoked nature would reflect something of an Asian aesthetic.

The day of the conference was beautiful and amazing. Our goal was simply to talk about ANA worship and try to take steps toward its further development. We surrounded ourselves with Asian American Christian visual art (banners, sculptures, and flower arrangements). Of course, we had Asian American food for lunch. The stage background was a stunning ten-foot-tall triptych paper cutting depicting the "water of life" by Alice Helen Masek, a local artist. We were not a scattering of minority faces in a majority-culture worship conference—we *were* the worship conference.

The highlight of the day were five composer-performed songs focusing on the Asian American Christian experience. These songs were mostly from a songwriting contest we conducted in the lead-up to the conference. Here are some excerpts from the materials we used to promote that songwriting contest:

> ❖Do you long for an Asian American "voice" in Christian worship?
>
> ❖Do you long to express the particular hurts and hopes you've experienced in your faith journey among Asian American believers?
>
> ❖Do you long to encourage Asian American churches and ministries in their identity and calling?
>
> ❖Has God given you a gift for songwriting?

We invite you to enter WATERWIND, a contest to encourage and honor your work as a gift to God; to Asian American believers, churches, and ministries; to Asian American seekers looking for a connection between Christian faith and cultural identity; and to the wider church.

A song that expresses something true about the Asian American faith journey can touch people of all backgrounds and cultures.

Your song must be especially appropriate for use in an Asian American Christian worship setting, whether as a congregational song or a solo/ensemble/choral piece. That is, your song should express (whether explicitly or implicitly) something in particular about the faith journey of people who identify with Asian American culture. What are the particular spiritual issues, wounds, needs, joys, and hopes of people whose lives are shaped by Asian American flavors of:

❖ Generational journeys, achievements, tensions, and gifts
❖ Shame, face, obligation, duty, opportunity
❖ Self-consciousness, emotional reserve, low risk-tolerance
❖ Indirectness, deference, self-effacement
❖ Family care; family pressure to achieve and succeed
❖ Submission of the individual to the family or group
❖ The minority life; the bicultural life; the biracial life
❖ Interracial courtship, marriage, adoption, childbearing
❖ Non/anti-Christian family practices, beliefs, values
❖ Racism (as victim, perpetrator, and/or witness)
❖ The physical experience of being Asian American
❖ Losing/rejecting/rediscovering ancestral culture
❖ The sensations of pioneering, diaspora, sojourning
❖ Recent or distant immigration experiences and the circumstances surrounding them

...or other aspects of Asian American culture or identity, whether positive or negative? Which biblical stories, metaphors, and teachings might God specially use in the lives of such people? What's the specific calling for followers of Jesus in Asian American settings? What's God's particular Good News for those on the Asian American journey?

Our opening song for the day was "Do You See Us, O God?" written and led by Jae Ryun Chung, a 1.5 generation Korean American pastor. "Asian Americans don't sing enough about their pain and sorrow during worship," he shared, especially thinking of the pain of conflict and disagreements between generations and cultures.

> Do you see us, O God?
> Do you hear when we softly sigh?
> Do you know, we often cry?
>
> Come now and touch, O God,
> Creating in us a brand new song,
> Helping us to get along.
>
> We know that there's no easy answer
>   sometimes
> The pain is so much greater than what
>   we can bear alone.
> O Christ our Savior,
>   came to suffer,
>   loving to the cross,
> Gave us the hope to carry on.

© 2002 Jae R. Chung. Used by permission.

What is ANA about these words? The sense of deep emotion and indeed deep pain, expressed with considerable reserve and restraint. The viewpoint and sensation of being on the margins and perhaps overlooked. The longing for relational unity and group harmony, expressed in a collective voice ("we" and "us," not "I" and "me"). The acceptance of suffering as a given part of life and of the Christian calling—quite different from the western and especially American expectation of continuous success, prosperity, and comfort.

The hope of the human condition is not to be found in easy fixes and cheerful progress. From a Christian perspective, the hope of the human condition ultimately comes from meeting Jesus at the very place of suffering and loss. "I want to know Christ and the power of his resurrection and the sharing of his sufferings by becoming like him in his death" (Philippians 3:10). Is this not a perspective on the Christian journey that ANA culture can specially illuminate, in ways that can specially balance the otherwise good and welcome hopes of western majority culture?

Afterward, one participant told us, "I especially felt encouraged when I heard, 'Don't apologize for your culture or ignore it.'" That's where we are right now, still working on not ignoring and not apologizing for our culture. Waterwind was one small step toward that goal.

Crossings

In 2004, a year after Waterwind, and again at the American Baptist Seminary of the West, I helped lead another one-day worship conference. We called it "Crossings" and it focused on a dialog between African American and Asian American worship leaders. ABSW was the ideal setting for this because its student body has included a full and good representation from those two racial minority groups. Thus, the need for such a dialog was not just theoretical but rather a lived reality every week in classes, chapel services, and campus life. (As an aside, it happened that the Pacific Asian American Canadian Christian Education board of the National Council of Churches attended this conference in conjunction with one of their semiannual meetings, and their experiences there introduced us to each other and eventually led to this book you have in your hands.)

I had actually wanted the Crossings dialog to take place a year earlier. However, wiser heads convinced me to start with Waterwind, and so prepare ourselves as Asian American worship leaders to enter into dialog with others. We had to first convince ourselves we had something to say, especially before coming into conversation with a tradition as developed and powerful as African American worship. We had to prepare our *self-offering* at Waterwind before being ready to share it and also practice *self-sacrifice* at Crossings.

Each Other's Voices, Each Other's Eyes

Two of the plenary presentations were particularly helpful. Dr. James Abbington masterfully bridged for us the expanse between centuries of African American Christian traditions and the wider world of majority-culture western Christianity. He eloquently taught and reminded us that while African American Christianity has roots in western Christianity, it learned everything it needed to know about sin, salvation, redemption, hope, community, resistance, and reconciliation from its own experiences and reflections.

James Choung, a young Asian American leader then on the staff of InterVarsity Christian Fellowship at the University of California, San Diego, and now the national director of InterVarsity's Asian American Ministries, provided valuable insights from his experience in helping to organize the worship sessions at the 2003 Urbana Student Missions Conference. At that particular gathering—the twentieth since 1946, with more than 20,000 college students spending most of a week at the University of Illinois at Urbana-Champaign in the dead of winter—there was a special emphasis on exploring differing cultural gifts in worship.

As Choung shared, what they learned was that the most significant differences between African American, Asian, Latino, and Caucasian worship were not song selections or musical styles. The most significant differences had to do with *leadership styles*. African American leaders were confidently directive, eyes wide open, working the crowd. "Say 'Amen!'" "Touch your neighbor." "Can I get a witness?" Choung labeled this *exhortational* leadership. The Latino leaders were more *relational*, sharing a particular sensibility about up-front teamwork, interaction, and celebration. Working together, singing to one another, and sharing leadership roles, they brought a palpable sense of *la familia* and *fiesta*. The Asian American leaders focused not so much on leading worship as being the lead worshippers—an *invitational* approach. A typical posture might be eyes closed, indirectly inviting others into the worship moment. The Caucasian leaders tended to be *explanational*, emphasizing reason and understanding. They would explain song choices and highlight particular lyrics and meanings and why they were appropriate for the occasion.

It is tricky trying to describe cultures in ways that are useful but not stereotypical. The fact that Choung shared from the actual experiences and thoughts of worship leaders from those respective cultures (rather than from an outsider's imposed perspective), that the intent was to lift up good and beautiful aspects of each culture (rather than denigrating and devaluing other cultures), and that there was no sense that these characteristics were categorical or restrictive—all this helped keep such descriptions in the realm of archetype and not stereotype. Can we talk about such things? It is not easy. But when we find loving ways to do so, the benefits are great.

Talk Takes Work

At Crossings it was both a challenge and a delight to have African American and Asian American cultures in dialog, one notably expressive and one notably reserved. At one point, one African American presenter was describing the Asian sense of silence and stillness and how this could well be worth cultivating more in African American churches—to which someone immediately shouted, "Amen!"

During the day we had scheduled time for breakout groups. We used a group process technique we had learned from Eric Law: invitational response. The leader begins the conversation and then directly invites one other person in the group to share. That person can pass or share, and then takes the lead in inviting the next person to share. As invited people share, others must simply listen without interrupting. If all goes well, everyone eventually gets invited and has a chance to share, even those who are more reserved, introverted, or hesitant, whether by culture or personality.

For some of the African American participants, this approach was frustrating. How long and how hard African Americans have had to fight to speak up and to be heard! As the protest bumper sticker exhorts, "Speak even when your voice trembles." How many ways each day do so many African Americans experience slights and small offenses to remind them that others consider themselves more important and obviously in charge. Yet here, in these small group conversations, it was many of the African Americans who were in the power position of initiative and assertion, a power that actually did need to be carefully limited and constrained.

On reflection, the surprise of the day was how much the quality of the dialog depended on these two racial minorities interacting *as peers*, meeting at some distance from the majority culture. As peers, there was a freedom that comes from mutual respect that could be taken as a given rather than something that had to be asserted or defended. There was a freedom to be vulnerably and self-deprecatingly frank about our own respective cultures' weaknesses, whether that was "folks who know how to shout but don't know what they're shouting about!" or how much one could fear "bringing shame on my people." There was freedom to laugh at ourselves and be invited to lovingly laugh with each other. And there was a freedom to hope that in Christ, even these two groups, who are so very different and so often separated by dreadfully deep mistrust and animosity, might actually experience unity and joy together.

ANA Worship as an Adolescent

In my own presentation I developed a metaphor for some worship traditions, comparing them to teenagers. There is nothing wrong with being a teenager, but it is a transitional and often awkward stage of life. A teenager is growing in independence but far from grown, sometimes awkward in words and movements, and sometimes easily infatuated with the latest music, stars, and trends. A teenager is often worried about being accepted and fitting in, sometimes given to thinking that all would be better "if I could just be like _____." Teenagers are typically still not fully connected to their family and cultural heritage and history. Teenagers don't know all the family stories yet and are not ready to carry on all the family traditions. Teenagers are still quite tentative about self-identity, calling, and future. And there is nothing wrong with any of that—it is simply a stage of life to navigate, embrace, enjoy, and eventually to pass through.

That teenager, that adolescent, is ANA worship. (At a different event, the theologian Amos Yong heard me propose this metaphor and replied, "Maybe even further: an *adopted* teenager." I am still thinking about the implications of that.) ANA worship stands like a teenager, awkward and unsure. As with a teenager, ANA Christianity is full of energy and idealism, so that, for instance, at the most recent (2009) InterVarsity Christian Fellowship Urbana World Missions conference fully 30 percent of the student participants were of Asian ancestry (3,008 of 9,950 students). That is a lot of energy, aspiration, and vitality. But, as with a teenager, Asian American worship is more about potential, aptitudes, and opportunities than something settled, mature, and confident. And the future of ANA worship is still quite open and hard to predict. When you were, say, fourteen years old, could you have predicted how your life would actually unfold?

So, given this adolescent that is ANA worship, it should not be surprising that there is still so little in the way of a distinctly ANA voice and style in worship. There is no distinct body of ANA music. There are no identifiable ANA ways of gathering, forms of prayer, styles of preaching, customs for the Lord's Table, or defining biblical themes in spirituality and discipleship. We have largely not found our own voice; we're still just starting to learn how to tell our own story, and we've barely explored the intersection of our story with the Good News of Jesus Christ.

At Crossings we pressed the metaphor of a teenager a bit more, contrasting it with the mature grandparent that is African American and especially black Baptist worship, full of wisdom, settled in identity, and able to move, speak, and act with confidence. To have a grandparent and a teenager in such a conversation was a great blessing. I am convinced that the further development of ANA worship will depend in no small part on such cross-cultural conversations. It is only in conversations that we learn many of the things we need to learn, both from others and about ourselves.

Emerging Voices

What would it be like to have three people groups in conversation about worship renewal, each of these groups early in the journey of discovering or recovering their own "voice" in worship (thus, a conversation between three worship "teenagers")? This dialog, Emerging Voices, was a year-long project in 2005–2006 involving Native American, Naga, and Asian American worship leaders, once again based at the American Baptist Seminary of the West in Berkeley.

The Naga are a people group whose homeland is in northeastern India and northern Burma. They are probably the most predominantly Baptist people on earth, this after decades of fruitful British and U.S. missionary efforts. But, they have never accepted their political assimilation into India during the British Raj or after independence. A live guerilla war for independence continues to this day.

The Christian evangelization of the Naga included an overwhelming emphasis on rejecting ancestral culture and privileging western church culture, so that the majority of present-day Naga churches look, feel, and sound like western churches. This is especially unfortunate because the Naga have especially rich indigenous traditions of dance, song, and adornment, which presently get mostly left at the church doors. As we shared worship experiences with Naga dress, dance, and decor, and as we set and shared a Naga table for Communion, we were heartbroken to think that something so beautiful (and, I may say, so fun!) might happen in Berkeley, California, but not in Nagaland itself. The pressing question became how to help believers there take similar steps to embrace Naga culture in worship.

Emerging Voices was my own introduction to Native American followers of the Jesus way. It could be argued that none have had a worse experience culturally and historically with western civilization and western Christianity than Native Americans. And yet these dear brothers and sisters have found peace and joy through their faith in Jesus, Grandfather's Son, and they wish to explore further how to embrace and redeem their own culture and roots as a good offering to Creator.

To hold an eagle feather in hand and lift it up in worship to God—for some this might bring back too many associations with the worship of other gods and spirits. But who made the eagle, its astonishing abilities to fly, and its intricate feathers and wings? And what could be wrong with any particular feather that had never been dedicated to any other spirit but Grandfather's Spirit? To offer back to the Creator this small token of creation can surely be a fully pure and worthy offering.

Of special note was the attention paid by the Native American leaders to matters of protocol and etiquette. In one of our gatherings, these leaders had made the effort to obtain the names of each and every person who would be there (something like fifty or more) and then to prepare small gifts for each person—sage grass bundles, small plaques, beads, and necklaces. They called each person up by name and presented the gifts with words of blessing, taking as long as needed to so honor each and every participant. It was absolutely beautiful. How much could we learn from such a commitment to proper observance, care, acknowledgment, hospitality, honor, and blessing? Compare this to the observation my wife made after visiting a particular majority-culture worship setting some time ago, an emergent-style service in a borrowed worship space rather bigger than needed: "Everybody seemed to be there alone."

At one point some of the Native American leaders stood to lead a song but first paused to address the Naga leaders with these simple words: "This song is for the healing of *your* land." To have these two peoples together—neither of whom ever asked to be called "Indian"—to share about such suffering and losses on their ancestral lands, to acknowledge with deepest respect the death and displacement each had suffered, to find and hold together our redemption and hope in Jesus, and to pray for much-needed further saving and healing—it was a moment of truest connection and care. How could I even begin to understand the depth of heartache and heartbreak these my fellow believers carried for themselves and their peoples? Yet there we were united in worship and able to seek God's grace together for the healing of these peoples, these nations, and their wounds. (One of the most unforgettable moments was when one of the Naga Christian women led us in prayer, she at times fully screaming, crying out, pleading with God at length, in the Naga language, for God to bring peace and healing to the Naga people.)

Native American culture may be especially helpful to the development of ANA worship in that its present expressions are largely a synthesis from many ancestral cultures, and not a preservation of one or another single culture. If you go to any of the big regional powwow gatherings across this continent, you will probably see an opening parade entry of participants involving a lot of "leathers and feathers," then drumming circles, dance competitions, protocol greetings and gift-giving, and of course, maybe too much fry bread. This is not an expression of, say, ancestral Navajo culture but rather a shared expression of any number of tribal heritages melded into a shared culture that did not formerly belong to any one of them. Unfortunately, such powwows have some of their origins in nineteenth-century Wild West shows and other demeaning, coerced demonstrations of Native American pacification. But now they provide a vital setting for intertribal gathering, affirmation, cultural transmission, and celebration.

Can you see how the powwow model might help in the development of ANA worship? We too come from a wide array of identities and backgrounds, but we now find ourselves mixed and grouped together. We too have been variously exoticized, objectified, and pacified. Might we too find a way to create a new, composite, shared ANA culture that becomes a good gift to one another and to the wider world? Might ANA worship be an especially good way to explore those possibilities?

New Urban Voices

In 2006–2007 I helped lead another yearlong worship renewal project, this one based at my present church, New Hope Covenant Church in Oakland, California. New Urban Voices (NUV) was a project focused on worship contextualization in Southeast Asian American worship settings. After the Vietnam conflict, Pol Pot's Killing Fields, and other wars and displacements in Southeast Asia, several waves of immigrants have come to

North America: Vietnamese, Chinese from Vietnam (many were boat people who fled for their lives), Cambodians, Lao, Thai, Hmong, Mien, Tai Dam, Khmu, and others. Many came after years in refugee camps in Thailand, so that there are now, for instance, Cambodian American young adult church leaders who were born in Thailand and have never stepped foot in Cambodia. What might worship look like for these brothers and sisters if their stories and cultures were fully embraced and honored?

In culturally contextualizing worship, it is a beautiful thing when a worshipper realizes for the first time that God actually does speak his or her ancestral language. At one of our events, a Cambodian American musician described the experience this way, after translating a praise song into Khmer:

> This was the first song I interpreted [into Khmer] and I felt like, "I really don't feel like doing this. What will it mean singing it in Khmer because I really like singing this song in English?" But it was an amazing experience—because while I was singing it I was thinking, "Wow, God, I didn't know that I can actually communicate to you with these words"—because I knew what they meant. "We praise the Lord." "*Chnom sawsah prah aung*"—hearing my own voice saying it in Khmer and singing it was amazing.

Immigrant grandparents can have parallel experiences in discovering worship in their ancestral forms. At another NUV gathering, this one in Long Beach, some young adults used traditional Southeast Asian instruments and dance for some Christian pieces they had prepared. I well remember the beaming smiles on the faces of some of the grandparents as they heard the sound of a traditional flute being played by one of the young adults. It was not just the familiarity of this sound from their own childhoods. I could imagine them thinking, "They are not forgetting who they are. Here at church, in their worship, gathered in the name of Jesus, they are not forgetting who they are."

Unity across Generations

The New Urban Voices project led to a partnership with the Southeast Asian Committee (SEAC) led by Ken Kong, who is Cambodian American. At its March 2008 gathering outside Washington, DC, there was an electrifying moment of reconciliation and healing. One night there at the conference, a gathering of first-generation Southeast Asian church leaders gathered to pray over and bless the second-generation and later leaders who made up the greater part of the gathering. One first-generation elder, Chiv Taing, was so moved by the clear spiritual quality and intensity of the movement that he addressed the whole gathering. He stood and, through a translator, asked the younger generations for forgiveness. "We brought you here out of a lot of war and suffering. So we simply wanted to protect you. But now I realize we held on too tightly. We need to release you, to bless you, to treat you as full partners. I want to apologize to you, to ask for forgiveness. I see we need a relationship of full mutual respect, forgiveness, and support." These were the words of a Southeast Asian immigrant church elder to a gathering of mostly 1.5 and 2.0 generation Southeast Asian American Christian leaders. For a "parent" to say such words to his "children" was a true moment of Christian love and reconciliation. (You can view the moment at www.youtube.com/watch?v=D0QZFxq3YuM.)

Earlier in the service we had shared extended prayer, worship through music, and a celebration of the Lord's Table. Befitting the setting, we had set and decorated the Table in a recognizably Southeast Asian American style, using a beautiful embroidered tablecloth, cups of tropical juices alongside purple grape juice, embossed aluminum serveware that one might typically find at a Cambodian or Lao restaurant or home, artwork expressing ancestral memories, and of course, a low table around which we came to kneel and partake. For many there it was perhaps the first time they had celebrated Communion in any way that was distinctly Southeast Asian American. I would like to think that such attention to these matters of culture contributed at least in small part to the later moment of intergenerational reconciliation, as the older generation could see the younger generation's full and creative embrace of its inherited identity and culture.

The seeds had been planted two years earlier in 2006, in Long Beach, California, at the first Southeast Asian Leadership Summit (SEALS). There, first-generation pastors were specially honored at one of the meals, seated at the head table, and each presented with a special plaque and words of blessing. As they introduced themselves, they shared some of their stories—being imprisoned for their faith, emigrating under perilous wartime conditions, starting churches here in America from scratch, and so on—and it was clear that the generations raised here owed much to their elders, no matter how challenging the resulting generational divide had become. It was a living picture of the Fifth Commandment, "Honor your father and mother." To honor is not to fully agree with or to like or to even be happy with. To honor is simply to treat as important and valuable. And this the younger leaders did for their elders.

At one point during the New Urban Voices project, we were at a gathering in which I, a third-generation Chinese American, was deemed an Honorary Southeast Asian American. I exclaimed, "It feels like a *promotion!*" not at all to denigrate my own heritage but to honor and embrace the very special movement afoot there, as well as the especially moving journey of suffering, loss, and redemption being lived out by these brothers and sisters. Truthfully, there are ways in which I feel these Southeast Asian American Christian leaders are already ahead of Chinese American and other older immigrant groups in asking questions and exploring possible answers about ministry and worship as bicultural peoples. I am honored to find myself among them and with them.

Young Urban Voices

After New Urban Voices, New Hope Covenant Church in Oakland spent 2008–2009 on a project we called Young Urban Voices (YUV). We focused on the relationship of urban youth (including many of the Southeast Asian American youth in the tough neighborhoods around our church) to Sunday worship. One specific question came to dominate the project: Do hip hop music, dance, and culture have a place in church? On one hand, there is no question that hip hop culture has come to dominate the lives and landscapes of so many urban youth, very much including many ANA urban youth. "Hip hop is *everything*!" said one of our local youth when asked what hip hop meant to her. On the other hand, there is no question that any number of hip hop songs and artists glorify crime, violence, misogyny, and drugs.

But as with the virtually identical debates a generation ago over whether drums and guitars belong in the church, we've quickly come to appreciate that every style of music can speak truth powerfully. Negative associations are real and consequential, and must be handled with wisdom and sensitivity. But the high sound levels, aggressive movement, expressive energy, emphasis on improvisation, and sheer creativity of hip hop are surely simply one more kind of "voice" that can be used where appropriate in worship. (How many texts from the Old Testament prophets would fit a hip hop setting perfectly? How about Jesus' Seven Woes to hypocritical religious leaders? How about John's visions of the Apocalypse?) It was beautiful to see our youth write and perform their own spoken word pieces with beatbox accompaniment, and to see them imagine and perform mini-dramas that included breakdancing.

Perhaps the more subtle question with hip hop is the same question that squarely faces so much of the Top 40 praise music that has come to dominate so many ANA worship settings. The question is this: what does it mean to use a style of music primarily defined by commercially produced songs and albums? Most churches are small congregations that do not have professional musicians or professional sound engineers. Even professional recording artists would not sound so professional live; the sound on their recordings requires multiple takes, editing, mixing, and doctoring with sound modification software. Yet this is the sound both hip hop and Top 40 aspire to. What to do with that, especially in so many of our ANA settings that have high levels of amateur talent and aspiration? It remains an open question.

Meanwhile we have found that especially in urban immigrant settings, there is an almost overwhelming sense of cultural assimilation. Youth see their grandparents' and parents' world as old and bad, and urban youth culture as something new and good. Of course, this is North America and people have the freedom to pick and choose the cultures they associate with. Yet, as the church, it's for us to push back at least some on both personal and generational individualism. It's for us to cultivate a love for one's neighbors, even if those neighbors are one's own (poor, uneducated) grandparents speaking a language we don't even understand.

So the challenge is to find a way for our youth to make a good use of hip hop, while being comfortable with it at an amateur level, and while also finding ways to integrate their own biculturality as something good and beautiful.

Deeper Roots, Stronger Shoots

The third national SEALS event took place in 2010 in San Jose, California, with the theme, "Deeper Roots, Stronger Shoots." The idea was to give particular attention to our "roots" in ancestral culture and in family experiences and journeys. Close to two hundred people gathered for two beautiful, amazing days together. It always strikes me how visibly freeing and distinctly energizing it can be for people from cultural and racial minorities to be in settings they can call their own. Where else would you hear a Mien American young adult razzing a Cambodian American young adult about how "at least you guys have your own country!" Where else would you have a Vietnamese American woman preside in a worship setting and proclaim herself proud to be among fellow "*jungle* Asians, happy to greet each other with fishy breath!" and for a time not have to defer to those "*fancy* Asians who host Olympics and have car factories" (let alone have to defer to the majority culture)? To be in a large worship setting of mostly "us" is no small thing for anyone, but especially for those who rarely get to experience it. There at SEALS, the "us" included more than a dozen Southeast Asian American backgrounds, each with its own identity and story, but also cultivating together a shared identity and story.

For the final night of worship I was tasked with setting the Communion table. Since we were in a borrowed church facility and most of the leaders were from out of town, I had to get all the serveware, food, and drink from scratch. I decided to go to 99 Ranch Market (the local outpost of the largest chain of pan-Asian supermarkets). There was little time and it was raining hard as I pulled into the parking lot. I found a rack of varieties of sliced bread, all matched for size and shape but all different, which was perfect. So I bought loaves of coconut, taro (purple!), and red bean breads. For the cup I chose some of the tropical fruit juices. For the serveware I picked out some Chinese porcelain. And then I only needed one more thing: some purple grape juice. (I always try to include that when setting out other types of drink for the cup, because I know some people just don't feel right partaking of anything else at the Lord's Table.) Now, there at 99 Ranch, where would they shelve purple grape juice? Maybe they didn't even carry it, and that absence would emphatically make a point about Asian food and drink in relation to Communion. But they did have Welch's there—not in the main beverage aisle, but right next to all the Coke, 7UP, and other western beverages! And there you have it: everything I could tell you about minority versus majority cultures in majority versus minority settings, displayed in the way beverages are shelved at 99 Ranch. And there I was, literally navigating that cultural border, precisely while choosing food and drink for Communion.

Before leaving 99 Ranch I had also bought a small bag of rice, thinking to maybe decoratively sprinkle the grains on the Communion table. As I set the table we spread a gorgeous blue Cambodian tablecloth filled with pretty rows of embroidered golden elephants. I arranged the breads and juices I had bought, along with flowers and some art pieces we had. We needed a cross somewhere, but I had not brought anything to make one. But in a moment of inspiration, I took the uncooked rice, poured a cup or two onto the center of the table, and shaped the pile of grains into a cross. It was perfect: Jesus, the rice of life. (Later, an older pastor who travels regularly to a country where Christianity is persecuted was checking it out and said, "Hey, this is a great idea, a rice cross—so if the police show up we can just scatter it and they won't know we were worshipping!")

It was dress-up night and everywhere you looked you saw the most splendid traditional finery, the kind of outfits that usually only come out for big weddings and such. Some of the men chose to don Southeast Asian peasant outfits to add to the fun. The worship service rolled, strong and good. The moment came when I got to share some words about the Communion setting. "Jesus is too beautiful to be expressed by just one culture, or just a majority culture. Jesus wants to meet you in *your* culture, and does not want you to need a foreign culture to meet him." People came up, knelt, lingered, prostrated themselves, prayed, bowed, wept, partook. I knelt and prayed, rubbing some of the grains of rice between my palms.

Among the last to partake was Linda, a Hmong American woman, and one of the conference leaders. She was resplendently dressed, head to (barefoot) toes, in beautifully full Hmong glory: a vivid multihued red skirt, shiny embroidered blue and silver top, long black sash, festive headdress, multiple necklaces, and other adornments. She knelt at the table praying, palms up, bobbing. She was crying. I was there at the table with her. She asked for the mango juice, and I served her: "The blood of Christ, given for you."

Unplanned, she got up, walked to the front center, and began to dance, with gestures and movement from her heart, from her people, from her way-minority, war-hammered, fading-away (or hopefully enduring), forced-migrationed, patronized, paternalized, objectified, mispronounced, mocked, invisible, clumsily resettled, dismissed, neglected, preserved, treasured, absolutely beautiful, and completely precious ancestral culture. She cried and danced, finding this place where she could connect her Christian faith with her identity as a Hmong American woman. Later she shared, "The Lord was asking me to worship him in my Hmongness: to Hmong dance for him.... A good friend prayed for me and the first thing that came out of his mouth was: 'Worship [God] with all of who you are.' That broke me. I thought, 'How could I withhold my worship from the Lord?'" She did not withhold her worship, and her offering to the Lord became a true and beautiful gift to everyone there.

During the conference I wrote some fresh lyrics for a song we would sing together:

> Blessed be your name
> In the camps where my fam'ly stayed
> Where our hopes for life began to fade
> Blessed be your name
>
> Blessed be your name
> When I'm confused about my race
> When I'm upset about my face
> Blessed be your name
>
> And blessed be your name
> In the lands my people left behind

They will never leave my heart and mind
Blessed be your name

A Final Reflection

As powerful, beautiful, joyful, and really fun as these worship conferences and workshops were, I have to note that it remains a challenge to translate such experiences into actual, sustainable Sunday morning worship habits. There is a sense that such efforts are perhaps for special occasions but not for "regular" worship. Thanks to these explorations, I now understand that gap better, that it should be expected given the tensions of biculturality, the still-nascent state of ANA cultures generally, the large amount of unfinished (if even begun) ANA theological reflection and construction, and the sheer hard work all this takes in the midst of the already full effort it takes to simply keep church going week to week. I certainly know what that's like and I do not want to add unhelpfully to anyone's to-do list.

At the same time, these choices about culture and worship are unavoidable. We make such choices whether we stay pretty much with majority-culture forms or whether we do press into minority-culture directions. This is our responsibility and our opportunity. In the words of Terry Wildman (Ojibwe [Chippewa] and Yaqui), one of our Native American leaders for the Emerging Voices project,

> Don't rush things, but also keep moving forward even when it doesn't seem effective. Decide if you believe Jesus wants to be worshipped in the context of your culture. Is your culture valuable to you and your children? Is it worth preserving? Do you believe God wants it preserved? If so then your belief will find actions. It has been worthwhile, the journey for us [Native American believers].

CHAPTER 7

Wine, Grape Juice, or Tea?

I have a Christian friend whose grandfather was a pastor in a remote, third-world setting. When each Communion Sunday approached, this pastor would embark on a journey of several days on foot to the nearest large town to buy imported grape juice for the Lord's Table.

On the one hand, one has to simply admire and commend such effort and devotion. I have no doubt that God fully and gladly rewards every such effort by every such pastor. But on the other hand, we can ask: does Christian worship in such a setting really depend on access to imported foodstuffs? (By now, you will be able to guess my answer to that question.)

I have worshipped with Christians in Sri Lanka, where there is no tradition of cultivating grapes. I learned that many of these believers have adopted the practice of using a locally available grape-flavored soda for Communion—that is, a purple beverage that has no physical connection to actual vines or actual grapes. What are we to make of that?

It is true that the grape connection provides a link to the Mediterranean culture of Jesus and what he shared with his disciples, even if only via artificial flavorings and colorings. (For you chemists, 2,5-dimethyl-4-hydroxy-3(2H)-furanone is the usual artificial grape-flavor essence.) But is such an attachment to "grapeness" (and the corresponding non-use of perfectly good and healthful local beverages) truly helpful or needed? For many centuries now, Sri Lanka has been renowned worldwide for its teas—you have probably enjoyed them, knowingly or not. If Jesus were at a church in Sri Lanka and had available a foreign, artificially-flavored grape soda there beside a rich, fragrant Sri Lankan tea, which do you think he would choose to offer as his blood?

When it comes to worship in Asian North American settings and ways to set and serve the Lord's Table, what are the boundaries and freedoms? In what ways might ANA identity and culture be more fully expressed and embraced at the very place where Jesus nourishes us with his own body and blood?

In matters of culture, there are perhaps no more sensitive and important matters than sensibilities around proper food, drink, and hospitality. Why, in western culture, are cooked eggs generally associated with breakfast? Hard-boiled, scrambled, sunny-side up, in an omelet, or however prepared—eggs are generally served only in the morning. Why? Certainly not for any actual diurnal or nutritional reason. These are matters of custom and sensibility. (Compare the fried egg atop your dinnertime bibimbap, a signature Korean dish.) One day my wife witnessed one of our children putting soy sauce on her (white) rice. "No! Chinese people don't do that!" she insisted. Why not? Again, it's a cultural matter, serving as an expression of identity and propriety.

The food and drink we choose to serve at the Lord's Table are expressions of particular customs and sensibilities. I believe we have wide freedom about what to serve, far more freedom than we typically use or imagine, especially in the non-liturgical Protestant traditions that dominate the ANA church. Such settings have the widest freedoms of all when it comes to worship planning. How can we make further and better use of such freedoms? I believe that embracing and exploring such freedoms is a vital step for ANA worshippers to take. In doing so, we will experience God more fully through the good cultural gifts God has given, and also make a fuller offering back to God of those gifts.

A Short History of the Bread and Cup

There is no question that the Last Supper took place in the context of the annual Jewish Passover and the weeklong Jewish Feast of Unleavened Bread (Exodus 12:16ff., Matthew 26:17). However, the scriptural accounts of the Last Supper do not definitively describe the Last Supper as part of the traditional Passover Seder meal itself (besides which we don't know how similar Passover customs of that time and place were to modern practices). None of the other Seder foodstuffs we would expect are mentioned, such as lamb bone and bitter herbs. There are long-unresolved arguments for and against various interpretations of the texts, especially on how to harmonize the relevant chronology of events in the four Gospels.

In any case, while Scripture certainly depicts Jesus as the Lamb of God, preparing himself to be the last Passover sacrifice (1 Corinthians 5:7), the early church did not make other particulars of Jewish Passover customs an essential part of Christian worship. In the Epistles there is no mention, let alone emphasis, on using unleavened bread in worship. (The sole references to "yeast" in 1 Corinthians 5:6-8 and Galatians 5:9 are entirely metaphorical, as are the Gospel mentions—"good" in Matthew 13:33 and "bad" in Matthew 16:6.) While unleavened bread was central to the Passover narrative and remembrance, we have no evidence that the early church concerned itself with zymology.

Our only direct description of the Lord's Supper in the early church in 1 Corinthians 11:17-34 is concerned primarily with interpersonal relationships and community life within the local church, especially across class boundaries. The text makes no mention of Passover or unleavened bread. Paul cites the Last Supper narrative in 11:23-26 as the foundation and warrant for sharing the Lord's Supper. However, he does not actually tie the Last Supper narrative to ritual particulars as they were or should have been followed in Corinth. We also do not know specifically how the bread and cup of the Lord's Supper were served in relation to the larger fellowship meal that appears to have been a regular part of the church's life in Corinth.

Since then, church tradition has been divided, with the western church generally using unleavened bread and the eastern (Orthodox) church concluding just the opposite and always using leavened bread. Meanwhile, we do not know for sure whether the bread of the Last Supper was made of wheat or of barley. We do know that barley was the dominant staple grain of the ancient Near East going back into antiquity, and that the common bread of Jesus' time and place was made from barley. Wheat bread was more expensive and was more likely to be used by the wealthy (its higher gluten content made for a better-rising, moister crumb; but barley is more tolerant of poor soils than wheat). In the end we can only guess what Jesus actually served at the Last Supper (barley, wheat, a mixture of both, or neither? leavened or not? how baked and in what shape and size?). And even if we did have the paleoculinary evidence to know, Scripture simply makes no special point about it.

Which is all to say yet again: Scripture is barely *descriptive* let alone *prescriptive* about the particulars of form in the Lord's Supper. Scripture does not establish any ongoing and necessary connection between the details of Passover observance and the new institution of Communion. This new, specifically Christian chapter of God's work is forever connected with the earlier, specifically Jewish chapter of God's work, and in both chapters there is a particular focus on a shared ritual meal involving sacrifice and remembrance. But details such as a particular use of unleavened bread are not carried over, reasserted, or required.

In the following few centuries in the early church, the Lord's Table became a weekly observance, and it was largely separated from full community meals (though when, where, and why this happened we do not know). According to the documents we have from that period, there continued to be no particular regulations about the type of bread used. Mostly likely it was everyday bread taken from the in-kind offerings brought by the worshippers. It was only in the fourth century, after Christianity was first legalized and then made the state church, that specially prepared bread began appearing. Perhaps this seemed more fitting as the worship settings became much larger and the overall production values of worship services rose.

It was during the Middle Ages in the western church that the bread took a distinct turn away from ordinary, everyday bread. Increasingly, the sense developed that the bread should be different, more holy, perhaps prepared only by clerics, and specially shaped into wafers. This was the period in which laypeople were less and less involved in the actual acts of worship: the priests did most of the praying and often most of the partaking, to the point where laypeople might take Communion only once a year, and take the bread only. In retrospect, most Christians understand this was an unbalanced sense of the holy, excluding God's presence from the incarnational world of the everyday and ordinary.

During the Reformation, leaders such as Martin Luther, John Calvin, Ulrich Zwingli, and Thomas Cranmer differed widely in their approaches to Communion and their understanding of its theology. But all of them sought to restore Communion to a more central role in the regular worship experiences of laypeople. In terms of worship, the Reformation was a push against clericalism and a reassertion that worship is the work of the people (the literal meaning of "liturgy" in its Greek etymology). (Clericalism is ever a hazard—how many worship services in our own churches today are heavily dominated by the people up front? How many churches have fabulously talented and skilled lead musicians who too often leave their congregations in the dust, with numerous individuals standing as silently as a medieval European peasant listening to unintelligible prayers in Latin?)

In the U.S., modern science and the industrial revolution greatly changed Communion practices. Following Louis Pasteur's work in the 1860s, Thomas Bramwell Welch developed a commercial process for pasteurizing grape juice, which kept it from fermenting into wine. Welch was a Methodist minister turned physician and then dentist, and a leading temperance worker. He and his son, Charles Edgar Welch, tirelessly promoted "the fruit of the vine" as an alternative to "the cup of devils." While the Methodist circles in which the Welches circulated had long had prohibitionist leanings, the work of the Welches helped fix the use of what they called "unfermented wine" firmly into American Methodist practice.

The Welch's grape juice enterprise continues to this day, now owned as a co-op of grape growers. Its most famous product remains the purple Concord grape juice Welch developed, made from the American grape cultivar *Vitis labrusca* (first developed in 1853 and different than the historic Mediterranean wine grape, *Vitis vinifera*). This has become the drink commonly served at the Lord's Table in so many North American Protestant churches, including ANA ones, and very often served from manufactured trays in mass-produced plastic cups (with churches' attendant sensibilities about sanitation and convenience).

Meanwhile, the medieval move toward "special" forms of bread returned with the industrial production of Communion wafers, mail-ordered or bought from the local Christian supply store. Uniform, tidy, indestructibly fresh, and with a mold-defying low water activity, such wafers feature every useful quality except perhaps physical semblance to real bread. (In discussions about the nature of Christ's presence in the bread and cup, sometimes the joke goes that it's harder to believe such wafers are really bread than it is to believe they are really the body and blood of Christ.) Inevitably, some churches have returned to actual loaves, actually broken and shared.

By the way, it is unlikely at the Last Supper that Jesus' words about his body included the words *"broken"* (1 Corinthians 11:24). The earliest and best manuscript copies we have do not include the word "broken," and its use contradicts the point emphasized elsewhere about Jesus' bones not being broken (John 19:36). Nevertheless, I have been in many worship settings where the presider solemnly proclaimed, "This is my body, which is *broken* for you," at which time the people literally (and cleanly) break their wafers, with an audible, dramatic, unison "snap." On the one hand, this is a laudable act of shared devotion, ritually experiencing Jesus' suffering, perhaps in the sense of letting his skin be dramatically broken in the process of being executed or metaphorically "broken" by death. On the other hand, it is based on an inferior alternative reading of the text and takes one further step away from the natural sense of "breaking bread," which is to share it—individual convenience-sized manufactured wafers hardly need to be broken to be eaten. We have the freedom to create and use such customs as a dramatic unison "breaking" but surely should only do so with understanding and care.

I have not even mentioned so many other forms and practices from history and in contemporary use: the medieval use of a silver straw for serving the cup, or the use of a spoon in Eastern Orthodox settings to this day (and indeed, a whole world of special implements and traditions in Orthodox use); special vessels made from glass or precious metals and jewels, and developing into various special-purpose forms (chalice, paten, pyx, ciborium, monstrance [and a whole era of dramatic ocular devotion to the consecrated host], tabernacle, flagons, and an array of linens and paraments); the very wide array of different words and gestures for consecration and administration; and even into our own day with manufactured Communion trays, speed-fillers, and so on.

What a journey, from ancient Jewish table rituals to then-new Christian worship practices, from the Imperial Roman church to European debates over theology and practice, from inherited old-world traditions to new-world innovations made possible only with the advent of modern science and industry. Through it all there is a common thread: eating and drinking together as an act of worship tied to God's redeeming work in Jesus.

Freedom and Responsibility

We are free to use purple Concord grape juice served in disposable plastic cups for Communion—these products of modern, scientific, industrial, western commercial culture. We are free to use saltine crackers, supermarket matzos, or mail-order Communion wafers. But I believe we are free to use other food and drink as well, especially in the non-liturgical Protestant settings that dominate the ANA church landscape.

In comparison, in Roman Catholic practice the late Pope John Paul II approved and issued *"Inaestimabile Donum* ['priceless gift']: Instruction Concerning Worship of the Eucharistic Mystery" in 1980, as drafted by the Sacred Congregation for the Sacraments and Divine Worship (later codified in Canon 924, "The Rites and Ceremonies of the Eucharistic Celebration"). This included an instruction that the bread must be recently made of wheat and water only, and that the cup must be grape wine mixed with water. (The "recently" is a precaution against the bread's fermentation.)

While respecting the intention to stay thus connected to various aspects of biblical and church tradition, and indeed while truly admiring Catholic unity, discipline, and obedience, I myself wonder about having such a requirement in what is probably the largest worldwide movement on earth. In every Roman Catholic worship setting anywhere in the world, these foodstuffs and only these must be used in worship. Besides the cultural issues, there is also the medical factor for those people who cannot eat wheat because of conditions such as celiac disease and gluten allergies. The Catholic doctrine of "concomitance" teaches that Jesus is fully present in both the bread and the cup, so that such people can take the cup alone. But some are wary of the alcohol (especially for children) and so may find themselves deprived of eating and drinking altogether.

To my mind, the primary point of a table ritual is to convey nourishment and sharing, not to be a sort of museum display or docudrama straining for historical accuracy, whose spiritual value somehow depends on reenacting cultural details we could not fully recover today even if we needed to. Yes, we are forever connected to God's saving works in and through the particular historical experiences and practices of a particular people. We never want to lose sight of our connection to the Jewish Passover or to the Last Supper. Nevertheless, given our mandate to make disciples of all peoples, the centrifugal cultural trajectory of the church as narrated in Scripture, and our present grasp of God's creativity as manifest in all the good and beautiful gifts of our panoply of settings and cultures worldwide, I simply cannot believe that there is some quality of grapeness or wheatness (wait, what about barleyness?) that is an essential part of Christian worship.

Many bicultural communities are already used to applying some knowing precision to questions of origins and authenticity in regards to food. At the restaurants in my neighborhood, very little of what is served could be found in their supposed places of origin. We think of burritos as "Mexican food" but you would be hard-pressed to find one very far south of the Rio Grande, and certainly not the big, fat, meat-heavy variety common in the U.S. Pizzas with red "marinara" sauce and lots of cheese and toppings are an Italian American creation, not an import. ("Marinara" means "mariner" and originally referred to cooks on ships from Naples who incorporated tomatoes into their recipes. In Italy, "Marinara" if used at all would thus refer to some kind of seafood dish, irrespective of tomatoes.) And prepared-sauce-based stir-fried dishes finished with a fortune cookie are very much Chinese American, not anything you are likely to find in China. And on it goes. In all these cases, probably the least important consideration is some standard of foreign "authenticity" that culturally validates the food. Restaurateurs know better: their ultimate goal is simply to get you to eat.

So it is with the Lord's Table. The ultimate goal, it seems to me, is simply to get us to eat and drink together in Jesus' name as an act of worship in which we are nourished by his very life. Beyond that, we have wide freedom about the particular foodstuffs used and the particular qualities they convey. I once participated in a Communion service in which the presider had chosen a Japanese American setting, including senbei crackers for Jesus' body and hot green tea for his blood. As she consecrated these elements, she said, "We usually use grape juice because of its color—it's dark like blood. But today I'm using tea, *which is warm—like blood.*" It was a startling and moving breakthrough moment in which an ANA staple—hot tea—conveyed something true and freshly remembered about Jesus' self-sacrifice. Surely the quality of warmth, which we could literally feel right there, conveyed more than any supposed quality of historical culinary authenticity.

I mean no disrespect to those with convictions about using traditional food and drink at the Lord's Table. But here I am, a descendent of a people who (like so very many and even most people in the world) have no tradition of cultivating grapes or wheat, who actually do have a quite full and even now well-known culinary tradition, and who yet today need to be nourished by Jesus' body and blood as much as anyone.

Meanwhile I live in awareness of the wider world around me, a world in which there is a universal story about hunger and nourishment, need and provision, want and fulfillment, a world in which tonight numerically more people will go to bed hungry than ever before in history. In such a world I choose to believe that faith in Jesus is the one true and best hope for each and every person and for all of humanity. In such a world I come to the Lord's Table weekly, gathering with my brothers and sisters in the faith, not seeking some kind of authentic historical museum reenactment, but rather as a needy and hungry fellow human being, seeking Jesus' life as the sustenance, medicine, and feast for my whole being, body and spirit.

So, what are the boundaries for the food and drink of the Lord's Table? I have lost count of the times that I have pursued conversations on these matters and people's response has been to ask me, "So, can we use cola and chips for Communion?" (Why does that come up so frequently? It must be all the cola and chips we have at church events.) Although there is sometimes sarcasm behind this question, I think there is also an honest attempt to sort out what is and isn't acceptable in worship, and whether our everyday use of such commercial foodstuffs may or may not overlap with the sacred.

My answer is: yes, you may use cola and chips — *but only if there is nothing at hand that is more nourishing.* Cola can certainly be shared drink, and chips can be shared food. But we ordinarily experience cola and chips as snacks, as "junk food," widely considered unhealthful and certainly not as staples of life. On the other hand, out in some camping setting away from other ordinarily available food and drink, and perhaps with a heightened sense of hunger and thirst, cola and potato chips could indeed convey life-giving food and drink. I think of my own experience in 2004 at the top of Half Dome in Yosemite National Park, nine miles and 5,000 vertical feet away from anything not carried on our backs. I can assure you that whatever miscellaneous food and drink I and my fellow hikers had to share there were consumed with full relish and thankfulness.

Truthfully, the tension between the sacred and the everyday is at the heart of Christian faith and worship. How to bring together the holy and the profane, the religious and the secular, the hallowed and the quotidian? If we claim to worship and follow Jesus — God come in the flesh, God incarnate, God crucified and risen—how could this tension not be our full, weekly, and even daily challenge? So, when it comes to the food and drink of

Communion, we should not be surprised by such tensions and questions, these alongside tensions and questions specifically related to matters of race and culture.

I myself would find it much easier and much more reassuring to simply know what is the *right* food and drink to serve at the Lord's Table, along with all the particulars about what to say and how to serve those gathered. But, as far as I can tell, God really does want us to take responsibility for using our own lives, cultures, and creative gifts as a good self-offering in worshipping him. If I just knew the one approved online supply house from which to get the correct food and drink—well, that would make things simple and easy, yes? But if I have to reflect on all these matters of identity, nourishment, and community, and then take the risk of freshly leading worship settings that well balance the past, present, and future, and if I have to wrestle with the particular opportunities and challenges of ANA worship settings and the wider cultures in which they are found—that is really a lot of work.

Freedom is a privilege but also a great responsibility, and sometimes even a burden. Despite the greater work, I am convinced that burdensome freedom is our calling. "For freedom Christ has set us free. Stand firm, therefore, and do not submit again to a yoke of slavery" (Galatians 5:1).

Loving Risks

Every change in Communion practices for twenty centuries now has involved change and risk. Looking forward, if Jesus tarries, one might only guess what future centuries will bring in agricultural and social developments and sensibilities, genetically modified foodstuffs, adaptations to climate change and population shifts—who can say? If the food replicators aboard the starship Enterprise ever become a reality (you know, like the one in Captain Picard's ready room where he's always asking for "tea, Earl Grey, hot"), what will they serve if asked for "bread and drink for Communion"? Hopefully the computer will know to ask, "Please specify the culture and church tradition." But no matter what happens in the future, we can say for sure that people will still need to eat and drink, and Jesus will still offer his own body and blood as they gather in his name around his table.

Nevertheless, all must be done in love. For some who have spent their whole worshipping lives being served purple grape juice for Communion, it is quite possible that nothing else would ever seem quite right. The particular smell and sharp/sweet taste of such grape juice might be deeply internalized and associated with full and good Christian devotion. I am not to judge such an attachment and I am never to put such believers in a position to have to partake in a way that does injury to their consciences. (I will consider matters of conscience at greater length in Chapter 8.) On the other hand, there is no value in a "least common denominator" approach to worship, in which Sunday morning is held hostage to the most generic, inoffensive, bland forms—especially if those forms are rooted in the majority culture and my worship setting includes one or more minority cultures. One of the great challenges here is to find a way to distinguish genuine matters of conscience from matters of simple preference and habit, and of superficial mistaken beliefs. I suspect that this distinguishing can only happen with full and good relationships in play.

So the question is: can we take this one step further, to intuit that there are any number of ANA people for whom Christian worship would be well and better expressed if the food and drink of the Lord's Table conveyed something more closely associated with everyday ANA culture?

At my current church, we do regularly use purple (indeed, Welch's) grape juice for Communion. (Our weekly service includes both Word and Table.) But from time to time we set out a variety of beverages from which to choose. Since our church has a special history with Southeast Asian American culture, we often use tropical fruit juices—mango, papaya, coconut—as well as soy milk. But, befitting our Evangelical Covenant Church affiliation and its Swedish roots, we have also set out lingonberry juice as well. We typically serve by intinction, where people take a piece of bread and dip it into one or another cup.

Of course, this use of multiple cups compromises the sense of one shared cup. (But using individual Communion cups is even less shared.) I think of this as a transitional stage, where we share the several cups on a common table as a way of expressing our varied but shared backgrounds. Intinction itself is also something of a compromise. In our day and age, there is an extreme aversion to actually putting lips to a common cup with anyone except maybe one's very closest family members. But dipping bread into juice is, truthfully, somewhat contrived, and not really an act of both eating and drinking together. We are still searching and exploring together. These are all matters of both love and freedom, to be navigated and lived out in actual local faith communities as they gather and worship in Jesus' name. "So, whether you eat or drink, or whatever you do, do everything for the glory of God" (1 Corinthians 10:31).

Once a couple came to visit our church in Oakland and the wife was taken aback by what she saw covering the Communion Table: banana leaves. She was Vietnamese American and had associated such things with food offerings at Buddhist temples. For us it was one of our Sundays to specially honor the Southeast Asian heritage of many of our members and to meet Jesus through that culture. What's more, these particular leaves were from a tree that actually grows on our church property. In this case, this visible expression of Southeast Asian culture did not prevent this couple from returning to worship, and indeed from experiencing an extended season of healing and growth as they became part of the church. But I know the experience might have gone badly. She might have been offended and scandalized or simply confused enough to not return. Such explorations and expressions are always a risk and there is no guaranteed safe practice.

I remember myself visiting a majority-culture church that aspired to an especially casual, suburban, baby boomer vibe. Communion consisted of an individual-portion package of wafer and cup together that reminded one of fast-food condiments more than anything, especially when they were passed around casually and hurriedly on disposable plastic trays at the end of a service that had already gone on past full length. I think I actually did take some small offense, my conscience pricked by what felt like consumer culture going a little too far. As with the banana leaves, it's not a question of validity but a question of the particular people there to worship using particular cultural forms, and how those forms helped them to worship or not.

In light of other examples of flexibility and change in worship forms, I wonder why purple grape juice has such a seeming lock on the practice of so many of our churches. (It is common in only some traditions in North America and New Zealand.) The main reason is probably the longstanding abstinent position on alcohol in some traditions, especially among some Baptist, Pentecostal, Church of Christ, and Holiness groups. (I lived in Texas for some years, where Baptists are prominent. Up to the late 1980s there were still "Blue Laws" on the books prohibiting, among other things, the sale of alcoholic beverages on Sunday mornings. The joke was that there was only one place you could get a drink on Sunday morning: at church.) Surely using purple grape juice is partly a matter of sheer habit and unreflective practice, doing things in their familiar, "right," traditional forms (even among those who would proudly claim to not be bound by prescriptive ritual).

There is perhaps the thought that Jesus somehow commanded the use of a grape-based beverage, perhaps in connection to something (what?) about the Passover, and that Welch's fulfills that commandment. (As I have tried to show, any such connection is superficial at best.) There is the useful physical property of a dark, staining color evoking associations with blood. There is,

I think, the strong taste of a not-that-common beverage (how many adults regularly drink purple grape juice?), which gives it a ritual sense of being special and sacred. There is also the lack of the kind of scholarship and authority needed to validate change: we don't really know if we can use anything else, or what our options are, or what permission we have or need for such change. In reality, a good many worshippers who are used to purple grape juice simply would not feel right partaking of anything else, even after explanations and reasons have been given with care and skill by responsible and proper leaders. Such convictions must be lovingly respected.

What there is *not* is an actual moral, biblical, or theological reason why we must forever and always use purple grape juice. We may choose to do so, but we do not *have* to. And, as I have tried to argue, there are actually good reasons culturally to explore other forms. I believe the ANA church has both the freedom and the need for such explorations with this and other forms in worship. Love, in this case, includes being willing to question common practices, not just taking the easy way by perpetuating them out of sheer habit. Love takes risks.

Thanksgiving Dinner or Wedding Banquet?

The practice in so many ANA worship settings of using purple grape juice and some kind of unleavened cracker or wafer is in part a question of whether the Lord's Table needs to be associated with just these particular elements, or whether indeed any local foodstuffs can be served for Communion. So far I have argued that we have the freedom to use any foodstuffs, and indeed that local foodstuffs that more directly convey everyday nourishment are especially worth considering.

Perhaps it would help to reflect on other familiar ritual foods. The U.S. holiday of Thanksgiving has become intimately associated with a centerpiece dish of whole roast turkey. In 1943

Norman Rockwell painted what have become perhaps his most famous images, the "Four Freedoms" taken from President Franklin Roosevelt's 1941 inaugural address: freedom of speech, freedom of worship, freedom from fear, and freedom from want. This last painting, "Freedom from Want," features an iconic Thanksgiving dinner, with a grandmother bringing to the table an immense and gloriously roasted turkey, her extended family aglow with anticipation and delight.

Poultry turkeys are indeed indigenous to North America. They may have been prepared and served at the 1578 celebration by the explorer Martin Frobisher in what is now Newfoundland and Labrador. Governor William Bradford mentioned turkeys among the game shared in the 1621 feast at Plymouth Plantation in what became Massachusetts. As much as the North American turkey industry would surely like us to all buy and roast turkeys throughout the year, we may hope they are glad to have at least this one holiday (and, actually, Christmas turkeys as well) all to themselves.

Can you celebrate a U.S. Thanksgiving without turkey? In my own Chinese/Cantonese American family, the turkey almost always shows up, even though many first-generation Chinese Americans really don't like turkey, considering it too coarse and strong-flavored. Nevertheless, how many U.S. expatriates, soldiers and sailors away on duty, and missionaries treasure any opportunity on Thanksgiving to share a taste of real turkey and perhaps a dollop of cranberry sauce? The STS-126 flight of the Space Shuttle Endeavour was launched on November 14, 2008, and not scheduled to return until after the Thanksgiving holiday. Among its stores were turkey, candied yams, and stuffing so that its astronauts could have a Thanksgiving dinner in orbit.

For this particular holiday and meal, turkey is the centerpiece. You can roast the world's most scrumptious chicken, goose, or duck; or serve beef rib roast, rack of lamb, or pork ribs; or prepare the most exquisite vegetarian creation. But no matter how yummy the alternatives, for so many it's not quite Thanksgiving without the turkey.

Now compare Thanksgiving with wedding banquets. In any given culture there is a full set of customs, traditions, and specific foods associated with wedding banquets. My own childhood included innumerable trips across the San Francisco-Oakland Bay Bridge and into San Francisco's Chinatown for wedding banquets at Joe Jung's, Golden Dragon, and especially Empress of China. Such special occasions deserved very special food, and it was all there, from the shark fin soup (now, thankfully, a waning tradition) to the Peking duck. There was even a curious sensibility around the cold drinks that were served: usually one bottle of 7UP and one of Belfast Sparkling Cider—an artificially flavored beverage that one oddly never saw or bought anywhere else. All this digested most happily in my mind and stomach as we drove back home over the Bay Bridge.

Decades later I have now been to any number of other wedding banquets of couples from any number of other cultures, and the food and drink has been completely varied and excellent. There is no one specific dish that must be served at every wedding, even every wedding of a Christian couple. I suppose an iconic wedding cake is currently something of a must in western culture, but even this can be of any flavor, color, texture, quality, fruit content or not, and decoration—as long as it is served festively and amply. The point of a wedding banquet is to eat and drink together in a fully celebratory manner. Indeed, the forms and details of such banquets are at their best when they are the fullest expression of the customs and cultures involved, both in tradition and creativity. All cultures have weddings and all mark and celebrate them in some way. The joining of two lives in covenant relationship is worthy of full effort and participation. But there is no single fixed way to celebrate something even so weighty and precious.

So, is Communion more like Thanksgiving dinner or is it more like a wedding banquet? Is Communion fixed in one particular cultural expression, involving some very particular menu like

Thanksgiving turkey and cranberry sauce? Or is Communion more like a wedding banquet, which varies across times and cultures, but which everywhere and always uses a shared feast to celebrate a new instance of one particular gift?

I believe Communion is more like a wedding banquet, with an unchanging function but complete adaptability as to form. Thanksgiving, and its whole roast turkey centerpiece, has no aspirations to become a transcultural export. It is rooted specifically in the United States' political, cultural, and natural history. The U.S. aspires to export democracy, but I have never heard anyone advocate the export of Thanksgiving and roast turkeys. What would be the reason for, say, Singaporeans to cultivate a specific taste for and industry in turkeys? There is no particular reason to do so. They have their own political, cultural, and natural history.

At the Lord's Table we dare to take seriously these amazing, scandalous, beautiful, shocking, unbelievable words: "Those who eat my flesh and drink my blood have eternal life, and I will raise them up on the last day; for my flesh is true food and my blood is true drink. Those who eat my flesh and drink my blood abide in me, and I in them" (John 6:54-56). And we actually do partake together of food and drink. What food and what drink should that be? With biblical heritage; church history; and the emerging, mixing cultures and peoples of each of our own settings, I believe we have wide freedom to celebrate and partake creatively.

CHAPTER 8

Conscience Matters

While freedom in Christ is a good and precious gift, it must be used in love. This is especially true in contexts of corporate worship, where our differing backgrounds, personalities, faith experiences, understandings, and callings give us each a unique set of sensibilities and matters of conscience about what is better or worse, what is good or bad, and even what is right or wrong for use at church. There are so many things Scripture neither commands nor forbids in worship, yet this does not leave us with a free-for-all. We are to use our freedom as a greater means to love and care for each other. "For you were called to freedom, brothers and sisters; only do not use your freedom as an opportunity for self-indulgence, but through love become slaves to one another" (Galatians 5:13).

For instance, how should worshippers dress for worship services? Should they dress up, dress down, or does it not matter? For the greater part of my own lifetime, worshipping at times in majority-Asian and other times in majority-Caucasian evangelical churches in the San Francisco Bay Area, I have been surprised at how quickly the decorum has changed. Ties and suits and skirts or dresses have largely been displaced by distinctly casual wear. (This has been tied in part to the Silicon Valley culture as it has developed here, where the emphasis is on ideas and performance over appearances and conformity. The joke is that if you see a man here in a suit, your first thought is that he's headed for either a wedding, a funeral, or an interview.) I have been a guest preacher at scores of churches over the years, and I have to ask beforehand how to dress because expectations vary so much. My present church is distinctly dress-down. And all this is fine. Meanwhile, I fully expect the fashion pendulum to swing again in my lifetime, perhaps more than once.

The question, of course, is not one of some kind of fixed Christian dress code. Rather, the question is what best helps me, myself, to worship (the rule of self-offering), as well as what best helps my fellow worshippers (the rule of self-sacrifice, even if this means putting on a coat and tie!). To dress up is fine if it is my way of offering my best to God; to dress down is fine if it is my way of coming to God just as I am, without pretense—as long as neither discomfits my neighbor or is a distraction to worship. We are called to love and freedom.

Not Commanded or Forbidden

During the Reformation, matters that are neither commanded nor forbidden in Scripture became a matter of major debate. (The technical term for such things is *adiaphora*, meaning "indifferent things.") Some Reformers, especially in what became the Lutheran and Anglican traditions, took the view that anything not forbidden in Scripture could be used, even things inherited from Medieval Roman worship, such as priests wearing church vestments on Sundays and the use of prescribed prayers. Other Reformers, especially in what became the Presbyterian, Reformed, and some Baptist traditions, took the view that we should only do what Scripture explicitly commands and nothing else. The more restrictive approach became known as the "regulative principle" and the more permissive approach became known as the "normative principle." Where would you land between the normative and regulative principles?

The Regulative Principle

In the Westminster Confession of Faith (1646), which emerged from the Puritan Revolution in England, the regulative principle was stated thusly:

> But the acceptable way of worshiping the true God is instituted by himself, and so limited to his own revealed will, that he may not be worshiped according to the imaginations and devices of men, or the suggestions of Satan, under any visible representations or any other way not prescribed in the Holy Scripture (XXI.i, cited in *Creeds of the Churches*, ed. John H. Leith, Atlanta: John Knox Press, 1982, pp. 216–17).

Here, "visible representations" referred to the use of images in worship, usually in the form of paintings and statues. Not only were such icons and images not commanded in Scripture, they were said to (wrongly) attempt to confine the infinite to finite objects, thus creating idols in violation of the Second Commandment. Heaven and hell were at stake here, with Satan himself attempting to lure believers away from true worship and into grave error. All was at stake in not going beyond what Scripture commanded.

Nevertheless, even the Westminster Confession recognized that the regulative principle could not be followed absolutely, that in practice the boundaries for worship could not be kept only to the express commands of Scripture. So the boundaries were set just a bit further out:

> The whole counsel of God, concerning all things necessary for his own glory, man's salvation, faith, and life, is either expressly set down in Scripture, or by good and necessary consequence may be deduced from Scripture: unto which nothing at any time is to be added, whether

by new revelations of the Spirit, or traditions of men.
Nevertheless we acknowledge...that there are some circumstances concerning the worship of God, and government of the Church, common to human actions and
societies, which are to be ordered by the light of nature
and Christian prudence, according to the general rules of
the Word, which are always to be observed. (I.vi, cited
in Leith, pp. 195–96).

Thus, if believers are to meet together for worship, they need
times and places, even though times and places are not expressly set down in Scripture. Since times and places for worship are
"good and necessary" they can be set and practiced.
Conversely, some argued that the use of musical instruments in
worship was both outside New Testament practice and not
"good and necessary," and so should not be used. Elsewhere,
the Westminster Confession strongly affirmed Sabbath-keeping
in general and Sunday worship in particular, which is ironic
since neither is commanded in the New Testament. (You will
remember the story of Scottish athlete and later missionary Eric
Liddell, who, as part of this tradition via his Presbyterianism,
famously refused to run on Sundays for the 1924 Paris
Olympics.) You can sense the real wrestling involved with trying to follow the regulative principle: a truly admirable dedica-
tion to obey Scripture, a justifiable vigilance against human
error (remember, this is all in the context of the active, explicit
Protestant rejection of the Roman church), and the actual prac-
ticalities of life and worship.

If you have read this far in this book, you will have long ago
discerned that I am not particularly inclined towards the regulative principle. Nevertheless, to argue as I have for the fundamental freedom Scripture gives us in our forms for worship means
that we actually do have the freedom to follow the regulative
principle *if we choose to do so, and can do so in love.*

I have a friend who married into a congregation in the Churches of Christ Non-Instrumental movement. This movement has its roots in the nineteenth-century restorationist revivals, which sought to restore church practice as much as possible to its first-century roots. Since the New Testament never mentions instrumental accompaniment to worship, some of these congregations choose to only sing a cappella, without any instruments, every Sunday. There is no piano, no organ, no guitar, no band, no drums, and sometimes there are even debates about whether to allow clapping. My friend had most recently served and worshipped at a very large church that always had full bands leading worship. On arriving at the Church of Christ, she was initially skeptical and resigned to her church-music future. But the simplicity of relying only on voices, the perhaps greater sense of participation when less of the focus was up front, the evident humility these believers had about it all (never speaking ill of other churches' musical practices and never claiming theirs was the only right way that everyone should follow), and the stunningly beautiful singing all won her over. The regulative principle can at times be applied to good effect.

The Normative Principle

This freedom to shape and order worship with care and love has been expressed especially well numerous times in church history. One might expect that a fully liturgical state church tradition would be unlikely to express this balance well. But the Church of England did exactly that in one of its foundational documents, the 1563 Articles of Religion. Here is the 34th Article, as cited in the 1801 version by the American Protestant Episcopal Church:

> It is not necessary that the Traditions and Ceremonies be in all places one, or utterly like; for at all times they have been divers, and may be changed according to the diversity of countries, times, and men's manners, so that

nothing be ordained against God's Word. Whosoever, through his private judgment, willingly and purposely, doth openly break the Traditions and Ceremonies of the Church, which be not repugnant to the Word of God, and be ordained and approved by common authority, ought to be rebuked openly, (that others may fear to do the like,) as he that offendeth against the common order of the Church, and hurteth the authority of the Magistrate, and woundeth the consciences of the weak brethren.

Every particular or national Church hath authority to ordain, change, and abolish, Ceremonies or Rites of the Church ordained only by man's authority, so that all things be done to edifying.

This Article makes three points: (1) forms in worship can and should adapt to different times and places—indeed, if they do not adapt they will come into conflict with Scripture; (2) duly established forms that are not manifestly contrary to Scripture are to be followed, lest legitimate authority be eroded and some fellow worshippers be compelled to novel forms they do not feel right about; and (3) anything established by human (and not divine) authority can be changed for the good of the whole. This is a model of balance of structure and freedom, of continuity and change.

Many of the same points have been made elsewhere. Here is the point about variability, made in one of the early, definitive statements from the Lutheran tradition:

For it is sufficient for the true unity of the Christian church that the gospel be preached in conformity with a pure understanding of it and that the sacraments be administered in accordance with the divine Word. It is not necessary for the true unity of the Christian church that ceremonies, instituted by men, should be observed uniformly in all places. It is as Paul says in Eph. 4:4, 5, "There is one body and one Spirit, just as you were called to the one hope that belongs to your call, one Lord, one faith, one baptism." (Article VII of the Augsburg Confession [1530], translated from the German by Theodore G. Tappert in *The Book of Concord*, Philadelphia: Muhlenberg Press, 1959, p. 32; cited in Leith, p. 70).

Of course, "pure understanding" and "in accordance with the divine Word" are not matters of ongoing debate themselves. But in any case, the basic principle of freedom stands, even in a fully liturgical tradition like Lutheranism.

In practice, the pace of change in liturgical churches is vastly slower than free-church traditions would ever countenance. New editions of the Canadian *Book of Common Prayer* (the official, prescribed service book of the Anglican Church of Canada) were approved in 1922 and 1962, and the supplementary *Book of Alternative Services* in 1985. In the U.S. edition, revisions have been approved in 1790, 1892, 1928, and 1979. However, both free and liturgical traditions have to deal with many of the same issues around change.

For instance, English-speaking churches have had to somehow navigate the change of language from "King James English" to contemporary forms. In my own church upbringing in mostly nondenominational Bible church circles, I well remember the fairly chaotic transition from use of the King James Version to the New International Version. Those who have grown up with contemporary English versions of the Bible may find it hard to imagine the depth and intensity of the debates and controversy at the time. Who would decide and how? What was at stake? Local church pastors probably felt the burden of decision, but where would they turn for help in deciding? Without denominational authorities, they were left to ad hoc arrays of personally trusted seminaries, authors, and colleagues, along with their own reasoning and pastoral sensibilities. There was quite an extended period in which it was not clear at all that contemporary English versions would be deemed acceptable, let alone prevail. My point is not that a decision from on high would have been better or worse, but that no one can avoid such decisions about changing forms (here, the form of Scripture in translation).

To this day, some who grew up with the King James Version and whose prayers were shaped by its language still do not feel right addressing God as "you" instead of "thou." While "thees and thous" were not special forms in their original Tudor use (nor is such a special form present in the original biblical languages), over time the pronouns shifted their "register" higher to become terms of special respect. And such forms survive even in linguistic settings that are otherwise entirely contemporary, for instance in public offerings of the Lord's Prayer ("Our Father, who art in heaven, hallowed by thy Name ..."). To respect this—to not require some worshippers to pray in a language form they could not feel right about—the latest *Book of Common Prayer* in both its Canadian and U.S. versions provide for the traditional-language form as an option even in the otherwise contemporary-language services.

(This whole matter is linguistically ironic, because the older pronoun forms such as "thou" and "ye" were already fading when Thomas Cranmer produced the first *Book of Common Prayer* in 1549, and he made greater use of the more modern form, "you." It was the backward-looking Authorized Version of 1611 that used the "King James" forms and gave them what has become a truly astonishing new lease on life. Nevertheless, using the older forms then and now are matters of freedom.)

Given the emergence of the more restrictive regulative principle in Reformed traditions, it is notable that John Calvin himself, writing in the sixteenth century, actually affirmed the normative principle:

[The Master] did not will in outward discipline and ceremonies to prescribe in detail what we ought to do (because he foresaw that this depended upon the state of the times, and he did not deem one form suitable for all ages)…[B]ecause he has taught nothing specifically, and because these things are not necessary to salvation, and for the upbuilding of the church ought to be variously accommodated to the customs of each nation and age, it will be fitting (as the advantage of the church will require) to change and abrogate traditional practices and to establish new ones. Indeed, I admit that we ought not to charge into innovation rashly, suddenly, for insufficient cause. But love will best judge what may hurt or edify; and if we let love be our guide, all will be safe (IV.10.30, *Institutes of the Christian Religion Vol. 2*, tr. Ford Lewis Battles, ed. John T. McNeill, Philadelphia: The Westminster Press, 1960, p. 1208).

Again, customs are needed but they are not unchanging. They are to be chosen for the benefit of all with the guiding principle of love. Of course, the most loving course of action is not necessarily the most obvious one, and it is certainly not simply doing what the majority wants. But love will always embrace a consideration of what others can and cannot do in good conscience. Again, it would be easier if we simply had one unchanging form of worship, take it or leave it, it doesn't matter how you feel about it. But by leaving all these matters of adiaphora up to us, Jesus actually requires us to learn to love more and to work harder at loving. We have no choice but to learn about each other and care about each other, to both accommodate each other and challenge each other to grow, as appropriate.

Scripture is entirely realistic about different people feeling differently about matters that Scripture neither commands nor forbids. We are not asked to all feel the same way about how to dress on Sunday, or which parts of the worship service to feel most strongly about, or what postures and gestures for prayer work best for each of us. But we are asked to always act in love, especially if our conscience allows us relatively more freedom.

A Case in Point

For some early Christians, such matters of conscience showed up not on Sunday morning but at the dinner table: whether believers could eat various foods that some considered questionable, especially foods that had been involved in pagan worship ceremonies. Paul discusses the general principles in Romans 14 and specific situations in 1 Corinthians 8 and 10:14-33. Some believers felt that their loyalty to Jesus required them to stay away from anything associated with the worship of other gods, especially meat that had spent time at a pagan altar somewhere between the slaughterhouse and the meatmarket. Other believers felt that eating such meat was fine as an exercise in Christian freedom. (I myself wonder about this when I dine at local Chinese or Vietnamese restaurants here in Oakland, nearly every one of which now has a visible altar somewhere in the dining area, with food offerings and incense presented to one or another deity or spirit.) Paul carefully sets out two basic principles on these matters of conscience.

Do Whatever Your Own Conscience Allows
In matters not clearly forbidden, believers are not to judge each other or feel constrained by what other people (including other believers) would or would not do. Instead, we should exercise the freedom to be guided by that inner voice which speaks conviction or permission in our own spirit—our conscience.

> Eat whatever is sold in the meat market without raising any question on the ground of conscience, for "the earth

and its fullness are the Lord's." If an unbeliever invites you to a meal and you are disposed to go, eat whatever is set before you without raising any question on the ground of conscience. (1 Corinthians 10:25-27)

All who belong to Christ have the freedom to enjoy and practice things that other believers might not, as long as these are genuinely matters that are morally indifferent, and they can do so in good conscience. So, for instance, if your church worships regularly at a time other than Sunday morning (and, conceivably, not even weekly), I am not to judge that, and you are not to feel judged, as long as you can practice that worship pattern in good conscience. (This was actually an issue for Pastor Bill Hybels and Willow Creek Community Church in Illinois in the 1980s when they started their weekend seeker services and moved their "New Community" worship services for believers to midweek. Some accused them of neglecting the Lord's Day and such. But Scripture gave them that freedom and they made good use of it.)

Do Not Compel Others to Act Against Their Consciences
In the privacy of my own shopping, cooking, and eating, I am free to eat whatever my conscience allows. But insofar as my shopping, cooking, or eating involves other people (believers or not), I am to constrain my freedom so as not to injure the consciences of others. I am not to serve guests in my own home things that they could not eat in good conscience. I am not to be a guest in someone else's home eating something they could not serve me in good conscience.

I know and am persuaded in the Lord Jesus that nothing is unclean in itself; but it is unclean for anyone who thinks it unclean. If your brother or sister is being injured by what you eat, you are no longer walking in love. Do not let what you eat cause the ruin of one for whom

Christ died. So do not let your good be spoken of as evil.
(Romans 14:14-16)

A Christian friend of mine once found herself on the Nevada side of South Lake Tahoe while on a ski trip with a church group. After a full day of skiing and then eating too much at one of the many prime rib buffets there, some in the group wanted to hit the slot machines. My friend had been raised to consider casino gambling absolutely forbidden for Christians. "Come on," some of the group cajoled, "it's fun, it's no big deal, we'll just try a few dollars."

Now, gambling is not expressly forbidden in Scripture. One can make a case that it is unwise and that it certainly can become very harmful, but one could not make a case from Scripture that it is always and inherently evil. So, in this case, those in the group who could pull some slot machine handles innocently and without compunction were basically free to do so. But to coerce a fellow believer to do something against her conscience—this is precisely and expressly wrong by Paul's counsel, a selfish use of one's freedom and a real harm and injury to that fellow believer.

In real life, there is often a range of actual individual, personal involvement with matters of conscience, and a corresponding range of possible responses. (It may be against my conscience to eat meat offered to idols, but what about, say, shopping for other things in a store that sells such meat?) I myself grew up not listening to secular popular music and not dancing. (I may not have missed much since I came of age in the 1970s, during the heyday of disco!) To this day I am a "weaker brother" about secular music and dancing, and I choose not to participate in them because I personally don't feel right about them for myself. But this doesn't mean I don't think anyone else shouldn't enjoy them, or that I am unwilling to be somewhere (say, a wedding banquet) where others are enjoying them, or that anyone should stop enjoying them when I am around.

In the same way, there may be forms in worship that given individuals would not choose for themselves, but that they don't mind having others around them choose. You and I may worship side by side, one of us with hands lifted up and the other not. One of us may read aloud a written prayer and the other not. One brings a personal Bible and the other uses the pew Bible. One partakes of Communion using soy milk and the other opts for grape juice. Scripture does not ask us all to feel the same about particular forms, objects, or actions. It *does* ask us to not judge each other and to act in love. In general, if worship leaders clearly invite but do not force participation, if there is good ongoing teaching about worship forms, and if the range of worship forms clearly does enable true and beautiful acts of worship from a range of worshippers, these things should not be problems. In recent years I have been heartened to see generally more freedom in worship forms along these lines.

More about Music

Perhaps you are old enough to remember the full-blown debates over whether guitars and drums could be used in worship. Those instruments smacked of rock 'n' roll. For some, even folk music was too closely associated with a spirit of youthful rebellion, sexual promiscuity, the rejection of authority—the subculture of drugs, sex, and rock 'n' roll. I remember buying my very first contemporary Christian album (12-inch LP vinyl, of course), *Maranatha 5,* one in a series that emerged from the music scene at Calvary Chapel, Costa Mesa, California, and Pastor Chuck Smith's ministry. I remember turning up the wailing electric guitar solo in Gentle Faith's "Jerusalem" and being told, "If we wanted to hear music like that, we could just turn on the radio." I remember multi-church summer youth camps in the 1970s where guitars were preemptively forbidden, even though we longed to sing and share the new songs we had been learning. I remember myself sometime in the early 1980s actually being the first at my church to play the drums in the sanctuary for a service. I remember how risky, tenuous, and controversial it all was. (The irony of course is that rock music has some of its early roots in various early strains of gospel music!)

Now, just a few decades later, the Beatles are elevator music, and you can hear as much rock music as you like at national political conventions or at the Olympics. But history has a way of repeating itself. At my own church we have engaged our youth in live discussions and debates about whether hip hop music belongs in the church. On the one hand, so much of hip hop culture has distinctly unchristian associations and themes: misogyny, sexual promiscuity, casual violence, lawlessness, drugs, and gang life. On the other hand, it is simply a musical genre, and like all musical genres it is well suited for expressing certain meanings and truths. Part of hip hop culture has also precisely aimed to express a voice of social conscience among an oppressed population and generation. Think about the Hebrew prophets denouncing injustice, corruption, and evil— would not an angry rap with a backbeat be a perfect expression of such truths? How about Jesus pronouncing woes on self-righteous religious leaders? It would be a perfect match. Nevertheless, there are matters of conscience about whether and how hip hop might be used in church, and so the question requires care and love.

So this is the tension: how to exercise our freedoms to adapt and change our worship forms over time, while doing so in a way that does not injure the consciences of our fellow believers. It is a perennial tension—in music, one could find these exact same debates during the Reformation, when Martin Luther and others reintroduced congregational singing in the common language, displacing trained choirs and Latin chants. How could coarse, untrained singing in the same language of the street and market be holy and worthy for worship? Simple: by being offered to God, who is not like a fussy high-brow theater critic. God has choirs of angels and archangels and does not need to be impressed by this-versus-that slice of our tiny range of cultural refinement. We take ourselves and our opinions of this-versus-that style of music far too seriously, like teenagers for whom the whole world hangs on whether I like your favorite pop musician or you like mine. How different adolescence would be if all teens made it their practice to say only positive things about each others' music! As believers we are commanded to "offer to God a sacrifice of thanksgiving" (Psalm 50:14). How different our churches would be if we were simply grateful and encouraging whenever we saw anyone offering up such thanksgiving, no matter what form it took.

When it comes to exploring the possible use of Asian instruments, melodies, harmonies, and genres in ANA worship, it would seem that matters of conscience are not major impediments. Chinese Christian Schools, a K–12 school here in the East Bay and attached to the quiet evangelical Bay Area Chinese Bible Church, has a full youth Chinese orchestra, with butterfly harps, moon guitars, pipas, erhus, and such, playing both Chinese folk melodies and western tunes. There is no particular association of such music with worship in non-Christian settings. What would it take to incorporate more of such music into ANA worship settings? Probably a combination of factors: familiarity (past the first or second generation, how many ANAs could hum even one ancestral folk melody?), suitable instrumentation for congregational worship, and perhaps most importantly, a spiritual focus with particular power. I think of black spirituals, born out of the fathomless suffering of American slavery. Are there any genres of Asian music that can specifically and specially express deep places in the ANA Christian spiritual journey? Simply using Asian melodies or imagery has its appeal, but probably only at a mostly token level.

Opening the Door

I remember as a child being at a civic event that happened to start with a prayer of invocation. I was extremely curious about how the prayer would go because I was almost never around any praying done outside my home church and my family. A local clergyman stepped up to the podium, unfolded a slip of paper, and read his prayer. "That's not a real prayer," I remember thinking, having been raised entirely on extemporaneous spoken prayers (at least, those prayers outside Scripture). Looking back, I think I had come to believe that extemporaneity was a sign of actual, personal faith, and that anyone who had to read a written prayer (even if he himself had written it) therefore necessarily lacked such true faith.

It is probably part of human nature to equate difference with defect, to equate "different" with "wrong." This presents a special challenge for Christian worship, since (as I have argued) Scripture requires, necessitates, encourages, and essentially commands the widest variety and differences in worship forms, both in different settings and in any given setting as that setting changes over time. Thus we need to be specially skillful and careful in navigating differences in worship forms to include navigating people's differing sensibilities about what they can and cannot do in good conscience.

In Chapter 7 I considered our boundaries and freedoms for the bread and cup of Communion, and I just briefly considered music for worship. What might be some other cultural forms worth exploring for ANA worship? Given our wide freedoms for Christian worship, we can reverse the question: what keeps us from exploring all manner of cultural forms, including postures for prayer; forms of meditation (here one would need to be careful about matters of conscience regarding Buddhist-related practices, such as the use of chimes or certain forms of chanted prayers); all manner of architecture, furnishings, and decor for worship; traditional written forms (e.g., Japanese haiku poetry, or Chinese "four character" sayings written in large characters on red paper and framing an entryway); traditional forms of song-storytelling such as Korean *pansori*; all manner of dance (here one would need to be aware of some associations with temple worship); and ways of gathering and sending. Why does all this seem like such risky and unexplored territory?

Even in attempting this stub of a list, I feel like I am being restrictive rather than simply opening the door. What if you came to worship in ANA settings generally *expecting* to encounter creative explorations of cultural forms for worship? What is to keep us from making that more the norm than the exception? I think of all the energy in recent decades around arts and drama ministries in many churches, so that such creativity has become commonplace and even highly featured. We have everything we need in the ANA church to cultivate that kind of creativity in worship.

Meanwhile, the majority culture belongs to us too, and there is no reason we cannot use it to tell our stories and express our self-offering in worship. I love Jae Chung's song "Do You See Us, O God?" (provided in Chapter 6 and also in Part Two) because it combines a very simple western melody with lyrics that specially express something about the ANA Christian journey. The entire range of western culture and western worship is ours too to use, develop, shape, and further. The caveat is simply to avoid equating "western" with "Christian," especially in our bicultural journey.

The Challenge of Change

In pastoral work, I have learned that people actually do want to grow and change—if they are well led into that change. Let me offer some advice for leading change.

Understand Their Questions

Leaders might think that the most important thing to do with people's questions is to answer them. I have found that it is actually more important for people to feel that their questions are heard and understood. (Sometimes this involves helping them figure out what their questions are.) Early in my own pastoral work, I sometimes made the mistake of thinking everyone's questions had to be answered to their satisfaction, that I couldn't leave anyone with an honest "I don't know." I have since learned that people can live with unanswered questions as long as they feel understood. Complete agreement is almost never possible anyway, so it's a strategic waste of time and effort trying to achieve such unanimity. We also sell people short if we assume they aren't big enough to be "loyal opposition." What people actually cannot bear is to not feel heard or understood.

Educate from Scripture, History, and Reason

Changes in Christian worship need to be grounded in appropriate teaching from Scripture about the functions and theology of worship. As you would gather from what you have read in this book, such teaching would also include *unlearning* what Scripture does *not* say about forms for worship. Given the scriptural freedoms around forms, teaching will also include examples of different practices and approaches in church history and in different traditions, and the backgrounds and reasons for past changes. Finally, teaching will provide reasons for proposed changes and the meaning and purpose of any new forms.

Understand Differing Motivations

Different people are differently motivated when it comes to change. Some respond to needs for *coherence*: the need for reasons and actions to match, the need for things to make sense and to fit. (Much of this book is actually motivated by my coherence needs.) Some respond to calls for *compassion*: reaching out to those in pain or need, such as those who feel hurt by worship forms that exclude or even injure them. Some respond to calls for *community:* the need to care for the whole body, to make sure everyone is included and gets to be part of the shared life of the group. Some respond to a *challenge:* the call to do something hard (like invent ANA worship!), especially reaching people who seem particularly hard to reach (say, ANAs who have long ago written off Christianity as merely a western religion). And some are motivated by *commitment:* they loyally respond to the call to duty, without asking many questions or looking for a value proposition for themselves. Different people can have these different motivations and still work towards a common goal, if leaders can skillfully motivate them in these different ways.

Create Opportunities for Ownership

Having a hand in creating a change is better than having change simply imposed from above. Giving people opportunities to help shape and implement change is very powerful. For instance, what if you commissioned your youth leaders to creatively decorate and set the Communion Table in a way that expressed their sense of sharing and partaking, and further had them write the prayer of consecration for Communion (first providing them with, say, a Trinitarian outline to work with)? What if you tasked a gifted cook with preparing the bread for Communion freshly on Sunday morning? I will never forget one Lunar New Year asking a church member to purchase steamed Chinese baos for Communion. She, being quite the chef and gourmand, made a special trip across San Francisco Bay that morning to procure the baos from one of the top dim sum restaurants in the area. The baos were gorgeous and her skill and efforts were a beautiful offering to the Lord.

Cultivate a Spirit of Humility

Change involves presenting a new form as a preferable option to be chosen for various good reasons, but hopefully not as the "right" option standing in judgment of all other "wrong" options, especially if those options were exactly the way things were done in the past. Who wants to be left feeling like what they had been doing for years was all wrong? A spirit of humility around changes will go a long way to prevent unnecessary resistance. At the same time, such humility will need to be accompanied by resolve and conviction that the proposed changes really can and will lead to a preferable future.

For some adults, who came of age decades ago, the best they may be able to manage is an openness to change mostly for their children. "You can change things for the next generation but don't change everything for me." Meanwhile, plenty of younger adults and youth are every bit as inflexible about forms as their most rigid elders. They need to see a good example of adaptability and growth from their elders, and they need to be well led into experiences that will help them appreciate a wider range of forms. Appreciative visits to churches from other worship traditions, missions trips, and simply a respectful tone when speaking of other approaches to worship can all go a long way in helping cultivate humility ("our way *isn't* the only way") and so develop openness to change.

Consider a Both/And Approach

Often a both/and (rather than either/or) strategy can help. In preparing what became the 1979 revision of its *Book of Common Prayer,* the Episcopal church in the U.S. adopted a both/and strategy. The liturgy for the basic Sunday service and other frequently used texts were set out in two versions, Rite I and Rite II. Rite I was closer to the earlier (1928) version, especially in its continuing use of "King James" English. In practice, Rite I became most often used for an early service mostly attended by older parishioners, and Rite II for the midmorning service including most or all of the young adults, youth, and children. Nevertheless, even the Rite II service included two versions of the

Lord's Prayer. The same strategy was followed in the Anglican Church of Canada in developing its 1985 *Book of Alternative Services* (not a Book of *Replacement* Services). Old and new forms can certainly continue side by side. Honoring and even continuing older forms (albeit in much reduced use) can avoid the higher costs of wholesale change.

Don't Write People Off

People can and do change. Peter went to Cornelius's house and ate his first pork chop dinner (if indeed that was what was on the menu). Paul was a Pharisee of the Pharisees before meeting Jesus; later he called the circumcision faction "dogs," devoted himself specially to the care of Gentiles, and came to consider all his Jewish pedigree worth as much as "excrement" as a means of righteousness (Philippians 3:2-9). Jesus famously pushed boundaries and challenged people to think and act differently about the Sabbath, about relating to "sinners," about gender relations, and about what to consider godly and ungodly.

I myself have grown into more bodily expressions of worship than I grew up with, now regularly crossing myself in Eastern Orthodox fashion, kneeling, and lifting hands on Sunday morning. (The Orthodox hold the thumb, index, and middle fingers together for the Trinity, and the ring and little fingers out for the two natures of Christ, and then touch the forehead, sternum, right shoulder, left shoulder, and then between the two.) At the same time, I ask myself whether I would ever hold lighted incense sticks while praying Christian prayers. There is more incense in Scripture than there are people praying with eyes closed and head bowed. But holding incense still feels too close to what I was raised to believe was definitely false and spiritually dangerous, since it was how Buddhists prayed. I think I'd be happy to worship in the presence of Christians who could pray in good conscience with such incense, and maybe if I saw that more I might get there too someday. Meanwhile, there are so many other possibilities: prayer walks, emailed/tweeted/texted prayers, the whole world of different monastic prayer traditions, and new possibilities to create and try.

* * * * *

I have made the point at length that Scripture is not a cookbook for worship. It does not even describe one complete worship service for us, let alone prescribe a service in detail. Scripture is overwhelmingly concerned with the object of our worship (God as revealed in Jesus) and various functions in worship (prayer, praise, proclamation, and so forth); it leaves to our wisdom and care the forms, styles, and particulars of worship. But designing and leading worship is all the more challenging because it involves people we are commanded to love (and why would we have to be *commanded* if love were not very hard?). People have all different backgrounds and sensibilities about forms in worship, and we are to respect their differing convictions around matters of conscience. Before we can do anything positive in worship we must first do no harm. And this will take all the greater wisdom and care in cultivating something as new as ANA worship, this against a long history of countervailing habits and beliefs. Such pioneering efforts will often not feel safe. To pursue ANA worship is inherently risky because change is always risky. But resting in inherited majority-culture forms is risky too, like leaving financial savings in seemingly low-risk bank accounts that will actually be ravaged over time by inflation. There is risk in doing little (with little up-side potential), and there is risk in creative exploration (with much up-side potential). I believe the risk of creative exploration in cultivating ANA worship is abundantly worth it, if it is done with loving attention and care for the consciences of those involved. As John Calvin put it in the quote I cited earlier, "But love will best judge what may hurt or edify; and if we let love be our guide, all will be safe."

CHAPTER 9

Another Beginning

Adoniram Judson would have surely smiled to be there. But he would have also had much to wonder about.

I was sitting in a Sunday worship service surrounded by Karen (ka-REN, rhymes with "ten") believers with roots in Burma and Thailand. They had gathered in their regular room in downtown Oakland at the historic First Baptist Church. Their service bulletin and projected song lyrics used the same beautiful Burmese script (also used for Karen) that took Judson extreme efforts to learn. The service was almost entirely in Karen (classified as a member of the Tibeto-Burman language family). All ages were well represented in the congregation, from preschoolers to grandparents. About half of the people had some kind of Karen clothing on, in a wide variety of forms and styles. A youth guitar player had a casual Karen vest over his T-shirt and jeans. Some of the women wore full, formal-looking Karen dresses: long, white, with embroidered trim. The female pastor wore a Karen jacket that was more modern and western-looking. An older man had a three-piece suit with a Karen shirt underneath it. Others had Karen scarves, skirts, tops, or handbags; still others were dressed in completely western clothes. The mix of clothing styles seemed to be entirely relaxed and happily bicultural, free from self-consciousness, and without any obvious division by age or role. Any Karen visitors who walked into the room would immediately know they were welcomed, honored, and known.

As I sat there I hardly knew where to start connecting all the dots surrounding me. What did it mean to be at First Baptist, Oakland—the very church that reached out over a century ago to my own immigrant ancestors in Oakland's Chinatown a few blocks away? What did it mean to be in a church that sent later missionaries to Burma who followed in Judson's footsteps? What did it mean that this Karen congregation was itself hosted by a Burmese Baptist congregation, the Karen people being a minority group in Burma and now again in this country, under this roof? What did it mean that the small and aging remaining congregation of First Baptist itself had, in 2010, voted to join the nearby Lakeshore Baptist Church, and to transition the land-mark church property to that Burmese congregation? What did it mean that Karen Christianity is as old as or older than ANA Christianity? What did it mean that these Karen worshippers were more comfortably bicultural than any number of later-generation ANA churches I had visited and served in?

From the Beginnings til Now

Judson arrived in Burma in 1813, one of the earliest American overseas missionaries and the first known Christian missionary to spend a full career in Burma. Born and raised in New England, Judson's burden for missionary outreach in Asia led to the formation in 1810 of the very first American mission society, the American Board of Commissioners for Foreign Missions.

Judson's ministry life was nothing if not dramatic. On the way from New England to London to raise further support there, he was briefly taken prisoner by a French privateer ship enforcing the Continental System blockade of the Napoleonic Wars. He later married Ann Hasseltine in 1812, only two weeks before they set sail for Asia. On ship, his further study of Scripture led him to embrace believer's baptism, and upon landing in India he and Ann were baptized by immersion.

(They had been raised as Congregationalists.) Their first year, spent in India, was marked by the Anglo-American conflict of the War of 1812 and the eventual need to develop solely American support for the mission in Burma. On the way to Burma, in 1813, he and Ann lost their first child to miscarriage; they later lost a second child, and then a third died not long after Ann herself later succumbed to smallpox. Most of her two final years were spent living outside a prison where her husband endured brutal confinement during the First Anglo-Burmese War (1824–26), this despite his being a U.S. citizen. Working together in the midst of all these hardships, they had attained fluency in the Burmese language, translated the New Testament, and nurtured the first few Burmese believers.

All this happened before the greater part of Judson's visible success, which took place among the Karen beginning in 1827. The Karen were mostly rural and mostly animists (unlike the Burmese in Rangoon, who were mostly Buddhist). Stories were told later of how the Karen's own ancestral beliefs had led them to receive the Gospel readily. The effort was greatly helped by fellow American missionaries George and Sarah Boardman, and by Ko Tha Byu, probably the first Karen Christian, who became a remarkably energetic evangelist. Today, the greatest concentrations of Baptist Christians in Burma are to be found among the Karen and the Chin people of the Chin Hills. Alongside the Naga of Northeastern India, these are some of the most predominantly Baptist corners of the earth. (In contrast, among the Kachin [kah-CHIN, rhymes with shin], a fellow minority group, the large number of Christians are predominantly Roman Catholic.)

In 1834 the widower Judson married Sarah Boardman after the untimely death of Sarah's first husband, George Boardman, and together they had eight children, five of whom lived to adulthood. In time, Sarah's health failed and she died in 1845. In 1846, while on his only furlough back in the U.S., Judson married Emily Chubbuck, a writer of some note. Together they returned to Burma for a few years of shared ministry. Judson's own health failed in 1850 and he died aboard a ship in the Bay of Bengal; he was buried at sea. Emily was expecting their second child at the time, and that son died at birth, some months before Emily learned of her husband's passing.

Judson left behind the first complete translation of the Burmese Bible (first published in 1835 and still widely used today), and the first Burmese-English Dictionary and Burmese Grammar. At the time of his death there were about one hundred Christian churches in Burma, with perhaps 8,000 believers. Today there are approximately 3.5 million Christians in Burma, about two-thirds of them Protestant, with Baptists making up about half the Protestants. Each July these churches commemorate Judson Day on the anniversary of Adoniram and Ann Judson's landing in Burma. Judson Press, the publisher of the book you are holding, takes its name from that missionary couple.

After Burma attained independence from Britain in 1948, it became a republic and chose not to join the British Commonwealth. A military coup d'état in 1962 led to rule by a socialist junta, ending just recently with putative multiparty elections in 2010 and the installation of Thein Sein as president in March 2011. Westerners are more familiar with 1991 Nobel Peace Prize laureate Aung San Suu Kyi, who is the opposition leader of the National League for Democracy. She was just released in 2010 from some fifteen cumulative years of house arrest. (Her late father, Aung San, is revered as a military leader during the fight for independence from Britain. An earlier generation will also recall U Thant, the Burmese diplomat who served as the Secretary General of the United Nations from 1961–71.) Now, late in 2011, there are major signs of political reform: censorship has eased, labor unions have been recognized, and further political prisoners have been released. There is talk in the west of relaxing economic sanctions. U.S. Secretary of State Hillary Rodham Clinton made an official trip to Burma, the first such high-level visit in some 50 years.

In 1989 the military government decreed the change from the English name "Burma" to the older, less western-associated name "Myanmar." (The two terms are related and both predate the colonial era. However, "Burma" became associated with British rule.) The name change has not been recognized universally. The United States and Canada both continue to use "Burma" as a way of affirming the clear and overwhelming election victory of the National League for Democracy in 1990, even though that result was annulled by the military junta. The United Nations uses "Myanmar." North American media are mixed, with some using the convoluted but accurate description "Burma, also known as Myanmar." Today, poverty, corruption, religious repression, and political conflict still greatly shape life in Burma, and it remains the poorest country in Southeast Asia (the per-capita income in neighboring Thailand is approximately ten times that of Burma). If that were not enough hardships, the country continues to recover from 2008's Cyclone Nargis, the greatest natural disaster in Burma's recorded history.

The half-century of military rule in Burma has been strongly anti-western, which has included anti-Christian and anti-minority stances. Some armed independence movements have been active since the end of British rule, including among the Karen, amounting to a long-running civil war. Persecution, forced displacement and resettlement, and open hostilities have led to Christian migrations and refugee outflows to Thailand, Malaysia, India, and China, where refugees and immigrants often remain in limbo. And now a growing number have made their way to North America, as well as to Australia and Scandinavia.

In First Person

I asked Rev. Biak Mang of Myanmar Christian Church of Metro Chicago (American Baptist) to tell me more about the story of Christians from Burma who now live in North America. It is not a simple story. Mang himself came to study at McCormick Theological Seminary in Chicago in 1991 and completed two degrees there before earning two more at the Lutheran School of Theology. For more than ten years he served on the pastoral staff of Taiwan Presbyterian Church in Des Plaines, Illinois. In 2000 he began to organize local congregations to host immigrants from Burma.

Q: What is your own particular ethnic background?
Among my people, the Chin, there are various groups identified, mostly by different language dialects, so the Falam, Haka (Lai), Teddim (Zomi), Matu, Zotung, and others. I am Falam.

Q: Can you give us an overview of the American Baptist churches with roots in Burma?
There are two kinds of Burmese churches in the United States. The first kind is [comprised of] older Burmese-speaking congregations in cities such as New York, Boston, Chicago, Los Angeles, and San Francisco. Most of the members of these churches were born in Burma with mixed Chinese and Indian ancestry and tend to be well-educated. The second kind are the churches with members from the various minority groups, such as Chin, Kachin, Karen, Karenni (Kayah), and others. These groups arrived more recently and so have churches that are quite young.

The oldest Burmese church in North America is First Burmese Baptist Church of San Francisco (Rev. Yishey Latt), with roots in the mid-1970s and official recognition as an American Baptist church in 1987. It has a daughter church, Oakland Burmese Baptist Mission Church (Rev. Lone Wah Lazum); that church hosts the Karen Christian Fellowship Church (Pastor Aye Aye Thaw). In San Jose is Burmese Christian Community Church of Silicon Valley (Rev. Zauya Lahpai). There are two churches in the Los Angeles area: Adoniram Judson Memorial Baptist Church (Rev. Samuel Saw and Rev. Than Oo) and First Kachin Baptist

Church. On the East Coast there is Overseas Burmese Christian Fellowship of Massachusetts (Rev. Maung Maung Htwe) in Boston, Myanmar Baptist Church of New York (Rev. Myo Maw), and Calvary Burmese Christian Fellowship (Rev. Saw Ler Htoo) in Washington, DC. Finally let me mention Myanmar Christian Church of Metro Chicago, where I serve. This list is just to give you an idea. There are also many other churches, fellowships, and ministries in all different stages of development.

Q: How are the relations between the various groups from Burma? Language differences are a significant barrier between these groups. Most people from the minority groups do not speak Burmese and do not think of themselves as "Burmese." Furthermore, after generations of oppression in Burma, the minority groups are experiencing here their first taste of freedom and equality. So there is a hesitance to associate with Burmese-speakers, who are associated with the majority culture in Burma.

Within the American Baptist Churches USA, all these churches work with Rev. Florence Li, who serves as American Baptist Home Mission Societies' National Coordinator of Intercultural Ministries, as Asian Churches Strategist, and as a member of the Burma Refugees Task Force; and with Rev. Rothang Chhangte, Liaison for Burma Refugees. We have had national pastors' training events for pastors from Burma, and we also join in Asian Ministries events with other American Baptist churches. However, efforts to all [come] together as, say, "Myanmar Baptist Churches" have not been successful.

At least for now, the Karen and the Chin churches are focused on their own organizational and ministry efforts. Indeed, these efforts have been quite successful, actually more successful in many ways than among Burmese-speaking Baptist groups. The Chin Baptist Churches, USA, is currently led by Rev. Dr. C. Duh Kam, pastor of Chin Baptist Mission Church in Maryland. The Karen Baptist Churches, USA, is currently led by Executive

Secretary Rev. Saw Ler Htoo (who is also pastor of Calvary Burmese Christian Fellowship in Washington, DC) and by Rev. Tha Hgay, president of the Karen Convention. In July 2011 at Houghton College in New York, a Karen Baptist Youth Conference (cosponsored by the Karen Convention and by American Baptist Home Mission Societies and International Ministries) attracted more than 350 participants.

All those who came from Burma as Christians (and Baptists) share the same roots and a sense of belonging to one another. There is shared culture, food, and traditions. But subtle differences from differing backgrounds and cultures sometimes create major barriers. Those from the minority groups tend to be very direct and speak their minds. Those from the majority tend to be more polite (at least outwardly) but also more dominating, since they identify with the majority in Burma.

Q: In part because of political reasons, Christianity is still depicted as a western and even colonial religion in Burma today. How does this affect churches here in North America?

The population of Burma is comprised of many ethnic and racial groups. The Burmese-speaking group is the majority and others are minorities. Most of the minorities, such as Karen, Kachin, and Chin, are Christians. To the Burmese, religion and race are closely connected and intertwined. As most of the ethnic minorities are Christians, the Burmese Buddhists have treated these people as second-class citizens. They see them as being contaminated by Westerners. They see Christianity as a western religion as well as the religion of their minority groups. Even in North America, many Burmese Buddhists see Christianity as the religion of minority groups in Burma. So for a Burmese to become a Christian would be to stoop down to the lower level of a minority group in Burma. This adds to the difficulty of evangelizing Burmese Buddhists in North America.

[Author Note: While early Christian missionary efforts in Burma (and around the world) were frequently tainted by colo-

nialism and by conflation with western culture, Christians in Burma today have come far in taking ownership of their faith and interpreting it through their own cultures. Despite frequent episodes of religious persecution and ethnic cleansing by the Buddhist Burmese government, the Myanmar Baptist Convention is run entirely by indigenous leaders today.]

Q: Early western missionaries to Asia had a mixed record when it came to relating to the national and indigenous cultures. How is the Christian missionary history in Burma remembered today?
The feeling is largely that missionaries from the United States thought western civilization, education, and religion were superior, while third-world civilization, education, and religion were inferior. These missionaries came to Burma with the intention of saving lost souls, civilizing the uncivilized, educating the uneducated, and uplifting cultural standards. Since race and religion are inseparable for the Burmese, many missionary efforts were taken as a condemnation and attack on both culture and religion. Many missionaries encouraged early converts to abandon their culture, traditions, and practices. While some culture, traditions, and practices are not suitable for Christian life, some valuable ones were abandoned.

However, one of the great accomplishments of the American Baptist missionaries to Burma was their translation and publication work, including the first work of reducing some of the minority languages to writing. Today, there are plenty of religious books and Bibles for use in Burmese and the various minority languages, much of it currently being printed in Thailand and India. The first Karen Bible was completed in 1853 by Francis Mason, an English missionary commissioned by the American Baptist Missionary Union. A fully modernized translation, the Common Language Sgaw Karen Bible, was published in 2004 by the Bible Society of Myanmar (www.myanmarbible.com).

Q: What can you add about worship among some of the minority groups?

The Karens who lived in refugee camps in Thailand maintained their traditional worship manners from Burma, including their use of the Karen language. The majority of the younger generation, many raised in Thailand and now here, do not understand the Burmese language. When they arrived in North America, they continued their traditional lifestyle and worship manner in the church. For the older group, it is easier to practice their traditional values, lifestyle, and worship manner. For the younger, the longer they live in this western society, the more they become adapted to western lifestyle and thought. To maintain this younger generation, Karen churches introduced contemporary worship elements with praise and worship teams including guitars, keyboard, and drums as well as translating contemporary songs into their dialects (Karen has two main dialects: Panapu and Palakhi); however, they continue their service with their traditional worship manner. Except for the contemporary praise and worship program before service, Karen worship services in North America are about the same as worship services in Burma and in refugee camps in Thailand.

The Chin are somewhat more distinctive in their worship. While they were in towns, cities, and villages in Malaysia, they created their own styles. As refugees from Burma arrived on a daily or weekly basis, the church made special efforts to publicly meet, recognize, and welcome newcomers by having everyone clasp hands at the end of their worship service. This custom has continued here in North America. The Chin also have contemporary songs and music composed by native Chin people in Burma, and not just translations of western songs, though they have those too. Most of all, the Chin people love to sing at the tops of their voices. So the Chin worship services here are a combination of traditional worship services in Burma, new customs created in refugee camps in Malaysia, and western contemporary worship elements. A typical Chin worship service lasts at least two hours.

Q: Any final thoughts?

There is a strong legacy resulting from the oppression, discrimination, and racism that the minority groups experienced from the Burmese government in Burma. It makes those groups wary of other groups, and not inclined to work with others from Burma or sometimes even fellowship with others. So there is a journey of growth, change, and even forgiveness we will need to explore.

The Future, Once Again

First Baptist Church, Oakland, was founded in 1854, just a few years after Adoniram Judson's passing. It grew along with the new City of Oakland and eventually built its landmark Romanesque Revival building in the first decade of the twentieth century. When the 1906 San Francisco Earthquake struck, the church was the most heavily damaged building in Oakland. The church recovered and went on to hire Julia Morgan (later architect of Hearst Castle) to design its main sanctuary, large enough to seat 1,800. It was her first major commission.

The same day I visited the Karen Christian Fellowship Church in a fellowship hall at First Baptist, I also visited the Oakland Burmese Mission Baptist Church service in the church's main sanctuary. It is a magnificent space, octagonal in layout, with massive wood beams, large stained glass windows, and a full-sized organ built by the makers of the famous Wanamaker organ in Philadelphia and the organ at Stanford University Memorial Church. I could not help but imagine what it must have been like in the church's heyday: pews filled with well-dressed worshippers of European (including many of Swedish) descent, a choir in robes filling the front, a full complement of clergy and deacons arrayed on the platform.

This was a leading church in the tradition that had supported Judson as the first American overseas missionary. Judson had traveled to Burma, on the opposite side of the globe, to serve as the first documented Christian witness among some of the peoples there, most notably the Karen. Two centuries later, descendants of those first believers in Burma have come to North America and started their own churches here. Meanwhile, the congregation at First Baptist Oakland itself experienced a long post–World War II decline, to the point where its remaining members finally left the building in 2010 and are transferring the property to the Burmese congregation. Surely Judson would have been heartbroken at the decline of such a major church in his own denomination, and yet amazed and heartened by the persistence and eventual growth of the Burmese Baptists, who are now in transplanted communities, including these believers to the east of the Golden Gate.

In terms of faith and devotion, the Burmese service I visited was heartwarming, with adult participants of all ages; several testimonies; a variety of musicians for congregational singing and special music; and prayers, readings, and a sermon, all expressing a full and shared effort at worship. However, the service could not help but be heavily shaped by its setting there in the main sanctuary. The space dwarfed the congregation's size. The fixed, original layout of pews, heavy pulpit furniture (used by the Burmese church leaders), and massive surrounding structure dictated a formal approach to worship probably not so different in essence from worship at First Baptist when the sanctuary was full of Euro-American members. The setting could not help but reinforce what was not there, what used to be there, the culture of a time and people long gone.

So much of what these people groups from Burma are experiencing in their churches is similar to the experiences of any number of immigrant groups in the past and present. These churches are centers of social and economic networking, especially in helping with jobs, housing, and children's schooling. Immigrants find these churches to be oases of ancestral language, food, and customs. (Sometimes even this reaches it limits, as with some coming to the Burmese church from one or another of the smaller minority groups, and not having even one language in common with anyone there.) As the children and youth in these churches grow up as North Americans, their changing musical tastes, bicultural values, and transition to bilingual or English language preferences lead to evolving needs for adaptations in worship and ministry. (The Oakland Burmese church has recently started a separate bilingual service.) The relationships between immigrant churches and majority-culture institutions such as denominations develop with a changeable mix of caution and enthusiasm.

Over our lunch of fish noodle soup, I chatted with two of the Karen young adults, Cherry Baw and Ashlee Mooloko. (At dress-up night at the 2010 Southeast Asian Leadership Conference I described in Chapter 6, Cherry was in a long Karen dress greeting us as we arrived. Remembering me from my church in Oakland, she greeted me first by folding her hands and bowing, greeting me with a Karen "Sah lah vee." She then looked up, bounced her fist off her chest, flashed me an "all cool" sign, and said "Whaddup, Russ?" How's that for cultural juxtaposition?)

Cherry and Ashlee told me of how they did not think of Christianity as western and did not feel like they had to leave anything Karen at the door when they came to church. They told me they thought of themselves first and foremost as Karen, although they might sometimes think of themselves as "Asian." But they definitely would not identify as "Asian American" because to them that means mostly Chinese and such, especially those who were born here. They said they actually felt closer to Thais than to ethnic Burmese, although they still have many family members in both countries. They were well acquainted with the story of western missionaries coming to the Karen, and then the Burmese majority persecuting the Karens for being Christians, and burning their churches. For them, being bicultural included a particular respect for elders and a careful use of titles and names. Their sense was that the Karen and Burmese congregations got along fine, even though separated by language. Certainly both young women struck me as being content and settled in their identities and fully engaged with all the different generations of their church.

The long history of Karen Christianity and its experience of marginalization, forced displacement, and suffering have produced, it seemed to me, quite a strong sense of identity and unity. On the face of it, one might think that my heritage in the Chinese American church would position me to share many helpful stories from generations of ethnic minority church development. But I came with more questions than answers. Indeed, these Karen believers generally seemed to be more comfortably connected to their biculturality than I am. Now, I can predict that things will get more complicated as their next generations come along, gradually becoming less Karen-speaking, some marrying non-Karens, and so forth. But for now, it is a special season of long-forged unity and identity experiencing new freedom in a new land. I am so very glad for them.

First Baptist Church, Oakland had reached out to my people starting in 1870, and their efforts led to the development of my home church just on the other side of downtown, the Chinese Independent Baptist Church of Oakland. I have seen pictures of Mrs. J. R. Bradway and Mrs. Amanda Egli, two of the nineteenth-century women from First Baptist who led the work, both looking very proper and well-dressed. I have to hand it to them, going into Chinatown when it was a poor, dirty, drug-filled neighborhood populated mostly with bachelors. Now it is Karen and Burmese believers who meet in the rooms of First Baptist to pray and to plan their own outreach efforts. I think of the majority-culture urban settlers in Oakland's downtown, attracted by a wave of new condominiums and apartments developed as part of former Mayor Jerry Brown's "10K Plan" (which sought to bring 10,000 new residents to Oakland's core). Wouldn't it be poetic if it were these Karen and Burmese who found ways to evangelize their new Caucasian neighbors? The barriers to such cross-cultural evangelism are significantly lower than what Adoniram and Ann Judson faced in Burma in 1813. (This is all also right next to much of the late 2011 Occupy Oakland activity and gatherings. I think these friends from Burma could share some instructive lessons about protesting injustice, evaluating potential allies, and enduring hardships!)

As one observation for contextualizing worship, it strikes me that even one cultural symbol or practice can convey a significant, even defining level of meaning. During the British colonial era in Burma, there were violent conflicts over cultural matters as simple as whether Westerners would remove their shoes before entering Buddhist temples and monasteries. One of Adoniram Judson's most helpful moves was his decision to build a *zayat* as a place to spend time with the Burmese. It is a small, public shed-like building that serves as a roadside shelter for travelers. It is not specifically religious and thus provided a kind of neutral ground for Judson to meet with Buddhist nationals. Buddhist laypeople might discuss religion there, but it is not a place for monks to conduct formal teaching or ceremonies. To meet Judson they did not have to enter his home, let alone a church. It was a space they were familiar with and that they could approach as part of "their" world (this even after Judson abandoned Burmese clothes as what felt to him was like ineffective play-acting).

For the Karen service I visited, I could not get over the symbolic effect of so many of the worshippers wearing all manner of Karen clothes. Even when we were singing translated western hymns, their identity was clear. Thus it seems to me it is well worthwhile to think of even limited forms of cultural contextualization in worship. There is no need to wait for wholesale efforts. Just one song, or a tablecloth on the Communion table, or the serveware for Communion, or some projected images, or the way the worship leader opens the service can open the door to a whole world.

Adoniram Judson composed a number of hymns in Burmese, including one translated as "The Golden Land of Heaven." It provided the title to Courtney Anderson's 1956 biography of Judson, *To the Golden Shore*. I think of it in the context of this chapter's reflections on the continuation of Judson's legacy in the Golden State of California.

> I long to reach the golden shore,
> And the face of Jesus see;
> My soul, with joy filled evermore,
> Will sing His grace and glory.
>
> From suff'ring, age, disease, and death,
> He'll set me wholly free;
> My joyful soul, till my last breath,
> Will sing His grace and glory.
>
> Regaled by draughts of perfect joy,
> Before my Lord I'd be;
> My soul in bliss without alloy,
> Will sing His grace and glory.

In 2013, the American Baptist Biennial in Kansas City will highlight the bicentennial of the start of Judson's evangelistic work in Burma. May it be an occasion for celebration, reflection, constructive critique, reconciliation, recommitment, and further explorations of the self-offering and self-sacrifice in worship of all those who will gather there.

PART TWO

Expressions of
Worship on the Way

Introducing the Expressions

My wife and I have on our cookbook shelf several especially nice volumes focused on Cantonese American cuisine. This is the food of our own ancestry and has been a large part of our lives both growing up and to this day. Cookbooks such as Ken Hom's *Easy Family Recipes from a Chinese-American Childhood* (New York: Knopf, 1997) and Ellen Blonder and Annabel Low's *Every Grain of Rice: A Taste of Our Chinese Childhood in America* (New York: Clarkson Potter, 1998) are not only loving collections of traditional recipes, but are also valuable collections of stories and images of the place that is Cantonese-rooted Chinese America.

Wouldn't it be great to have a big, fat cookbook for Asian North American worship, chock-full of prayers, images, liturgies, scripts, songs, ideas for worship stations, stories, and spoken word pieces fully and beautifully expressing the journey of ANA Christian faith and worship? The day may come when such a collection might be possible—but we are not there yet.

What follows is a small collection of materials for ANA worship settings, all useable but meant mostly to help inspire your own creativity and artistry. In so many of our church settings we have become overly dependent on commercially produced music and other worship materials. While we can be thankful for the range and availability of such works, there is every reason to also encourage our own local writers, musicians, and artists to cultivate their own gifts and express their own voices and visions for our shared worship life.

The measure of Christian worship leadership is always and ultimately: how well did we help people actually worship? How well did we help them make a full and good self-offering in worship, and also make a full and good self-sacrifice for the sake of their fellow worshippers? How well did we do this on any given Sunday, as well as in helping nurture a sustainable, living, thriving worship tradition from generation to generation? In ANA settings, we perhaps need a special emphasis on our own locally produced worship materials, so as to balance the otherwise inexorable pressure to assimilate to majority-culture forms, voices, styles, and expressions.

What makes something in worship ANA? It can be something explicit, like a sermon illustration that names a favorite Asian food, mentions a recent Asian pop culture personality, or references Confucius. It can be more implicit, such as Harold Jow's song here, "Sandalwood Hills and Mountains of Gold." It can be more topical, such as my own song here, "Never Not in Need of Grace," which expresses the tension between dutiful achievement and salvation by grace. Of course, it could also be a majority-culture form, for those forms are ours too and they express true things about us in worship.

I think of the hymn "Lift Ev'ry Voice and Sing," often called the "Black National Anthem." Its writer, James Weldon Johnson, was an African American principal at a segregated school in Florida, and he composed a poem for a visit by Booker T. Washington at a celebration of Lincoln's birthday in February 1900. The words say nothing specifically about African America but has lines that resonate with the long struggle against Jim Crow and the hope of equality ("Sing a song full of the faith that the dark past has taught us," "Stony the road we trod/Bitter the chast'ning rod/Felt in the days when hope unborn had died," "God of our weary years/God of our silent tears/...Led us into the light"). I think of the especially painful chapters of ANA history, such as the Japanese American WWII internment camp experience and the Southeast Asian refugee resettlement experience. Where are the songs, prayers, and rituals that would give us a way to offer these parts of ourselves to

God in the worship moment, to meet God there and thus experience God's grace for such wounds?

I would like you to find the following examples all too few and incomplete. I would like you to be dissatisfied with what is available, and inspired and energized to go about creating your own ANA worship materials. And I would like to hear from you! Write me at worshipontheway@gmail.com. Also, you can see pictures of ANA worship settings and find useful links at www.worshipontheway.blogspot.com (see QRcode below); and you can add your comments there. Let's share further where God takes us on this journey of ANA worship.

A GATHERING RITUAL
Honoring Our Ancestors

This is an excellent way to open a gathering, situating a group and its participants relationally in both time and space.

Sit in a circle and give each participant a slip of paper on which to write the name of an ancestor he or she wishes to honor. Tell them this can be anyone, from a still-living parent to a long-dead ancestor. Allow a few minutes for thinking and writing. Then invite people to come to the front and share the name of their ancestor and some words about why they wish to honor her or him. At the end of their sharing, the person in front says, "I honor [the name of his or her ancestor]." The group responds with, "We honor [the name of his or her ancestor]."

This worship exercise is both easy and hard. The easy part is thinking of ancestors to honor. In the many times I've led this, with groups ranging from youth to grandparents, each and every participant invariably has at least one ancestor readily come to mind. The hard part is assuring people that the tears, hard swallows, and pauses that sometimes come with such sharing are also welcome. These ancestors are often people who made hard choices, sacrificed much, endured hardship and suffering, preserved important values, and made courageous choices, all of which gave us the gift of our lives and identities. Among these are ancestors who themselves may not have known and trusted Jesus but whose lives and efforts made it possible for us to know and trust Jesus. There is every reason to experience deep feelings when we remember these ancestors and share about them with others, so as to honor them.

THE LORD'S TABLE
Tatami Mat Communion

At the heart of Communion is eating and drinking together in the Lord's name, as a way of being nourished by his body and blood. But the cultural forms for the food, drink, dishes, table setting, and ways of serving are all matters of freedom and creative offering to God.

Genuine rigid Japanese tatami mats are amazing and beautiful but are very expensive and hard to transport. Inexpensive straw beach mats work quite well as a substitute. Use a low table for the Communion setting, perhaps with shoji screens, ikebana-style floral arrangements, and perhaps tea and senbei crackers for the elements. Of course, the first rule of tatami mats is that you do not wear street shoes to walk on them. This provides an opportunity for shoes-off Communion, a way of expressing holiness and reverence.

You can incorporate a shoes-off/on component to this. This can actually work even better than literal foot washing—for which modern Christians generally arrive with already-clean feet and no actual need for a rinse. But all still need their shoes on and off, and seniors especially can benefit from help with this. Have your church leaders stationed by stools alongside the tatami mats and help with shoes. What could be more beautiful?

Various Southeast Asian cultures likewise have traditions of using woven floor mats at home and sitting on them to eat. There is every reason to incorporate such customs into Communion settings. To do so visibly expresses both our welcome to Jesus into that part of our lives, and Jesus' welcome to us, that he is happy to be met and to give himself in just such a setting, to people for whom such a setting is specially familiar and welcoming.

SONG
"Sandalwood Hills and Mountains of Gold"
Words by Rev. Harold Jow, San Diego, California
Sung to St. Catharine ("Faith of Our Fathers")
Used by permission.

*For minority peoples, there is ever and always a need to special-
ly remember and preserve stories from the past—stories that
would otherwise simply be forgotten, even if only innocently in
majority-culture settings. Here is a hymn text about sandalwood
hills (Hawaii) and mountains of gold (California), both of which
loom so large in the ANA journey.*

*Pastor Jow grew up in the Bay Area in the 1930s and '40s,
graduating from University of California, Berkeley; San
Francisco Theological Seminary; and Princeton Seminary. As a
Chinese American with Japanese American friends, he volun-
teered to serve as a youth pastor at the Japanese American
Relocation Camp at Topaz, Utah.*

*About this song, he says, "My hymn sums up my thoughts and
experiences during a critical time for Asians in our country. It
was composed around 1975 to celebrate the sixtieth anniversary
of the United Church of Christ on Judd Street in Honolulu,
where I was the pastor. The words came to me at night when it
was very quiet in the manse where we lived."*

Our fathers sailed to this land long ago
Sandalwood Hills and Mountains of Gold
They sought for work and their fortunes to earn
Then to their homes and village return
    Sandalwood Hills and Mountains of Gold
    We thank you, Lord, for folks of old!

Here on these shores they did labor with zeal
In mines, on farms, in camps, and in fields
Though oft forgotten, alone and oppressed
Yet they endured, pursuing their quest
> Sandalwood Hills and Mountains of Gold
> We thank you, Lord, for hope so bold!

Here 'neath the soil they lie in their rest,
Their work all done, their children so blest
Wisdom and service, devotion and truth
Flowed from their toil, your goodness to prove
> Sandalwood Hills and Mountains of Gold,
> We thank you, Lord, for lives to mold!

And we their children do gratefully share
Your gifts of life, your love and your care
Our blessings, fortunes, our heritage, skills,
We owe to them, we owe to you
> Sandalwood Hills and Mountains of Gold,
> We thank you, Lord, for faith to hold!

This is our country, our home, our domain,
Keep us e'er humble, trusting, restrained
Forgive our failings, renew us yet still,
Christ be our guide, your Spirit to fill
> Sandalwood Hills and Mountains of Gold,
> We thank you, Lord, ten thousandfold!

SONG
"God Is So Good," in many languages

Take a familiar chorus like this and recruit as many of your bilingual or multilingual church members as possible to translate it into non-English languages they know. Then when it comes time to lead the song in the worship service, line up those members and have them lead it one after the other, in those languages, with the various translations printed or projected.

Once when we did this on a Sunday morning, one of our members found himself in tears, hearing a language from his childhood being lifted up in praise to God. We so easily divide and segment different parts of our lives. But making a full self-offering in worship surely includes reconnecting all the parts of our lives in worship. For those with immigrant roots in living memory, this usually includes first languages, languages heard in childhood, and/or ancestral languages.

ENGLISH
God is so good, God is so good, God is so good,
He's so good to me.

KOREAN
Jo oo shin Ha Na Nim...(x3)
Na yeh Ha Na Nim.

KHMER (Cambodian)
Preah troung la-aw nahs...(x3)
Troung la-aw nahs dawl knyom.

TAGALOG
Dios ay tapat...(x3)
Siya'y tapat sa 'kin.

LAO
Prachao song khun khwam dee...(x3)
Song khun khwam dee phra-ong.

TAIWANESE
Shoun-de jin ho...(x3)
E dwee wa jin ho.

KAREN
Ywa Nay Hgay Wel...(x3)
Hgay Wel Lel Ya Hgaw.

CHIN (FALAM)
Bawi pa a ttha...(x3)
Ka hrang ah a ttha

KACHIN
Shi mai ka-ja...(x3)
Ka-ja htum "Ka rai."

BURMESE
Kawng myat pe ih...(x3)
Ko daw kawng myat ih.

SONG

"Never Not in Need of Grace"
by Russell Yee

One Sunday two men went to church to pray.

The first man was feeling pretty good about himself. He figured that whatever was wrong with this world, it wasn't his fault, because he lived such a good life. So he prayed: "God, thank you I'm not like other people. I work hard, I do everything I'm supposed to do (and a little more), I stay in control and don't mess up, I keep it all together. Thank you, God." And he went on like this.

The other man was different. He knew he was no better than other people. Oh, he was a law-abiding citizen; he paid his taxes and he even helped others pay their taxes too. But in his heart he knew his thoughts and desires were not pure, he worried about all the wrong things, and his heart was not whole. So when he prayed, he simply said, "God, have mercy on me, a sinner."

That day, only one of these men went home right with God. I want to be like that man.

> *Verse 1*
> I work really hard and I rarely complain.
> I try not to show it when I'm in pain.
> I plan what I say, and I keep to my space;
> > But I'm never not in need of grace, no,
> > I'm never not in need of grace.
>
> *Chorus*
> Please save my soul not just my face—
> I'm never not in need of grace.
> Not "Sometimes," "Maybe," "Just in Case"—
> No, I'm never, never, ever not in need of grace.

Verse 2
I optimize things and I don't like to wait,
I watch, consider, and calculate.
I usually live at my maximum pace;
> But I'm never not in need of grace, no,
> I'm never not in need of grace.

Verse 3
I never make waves and I pull my own weight.
All favors I always reciprocate.
I honor my parents and honor my race;
> But I'm never not in need of grace, no,
> I'm never not in need of grace.

Bridge
Dearest Jesus, how I need you—
At my worst and at my best!
Save me from myself, I plead you!
Only you can give me rest!

Keyboard audio version available at:
www.youtube.com/watch? v=0mo2wKe4WFo

Full music score available at:
www.worshipontheway.blogspot.com

SONG

"Do You See Us, O God?"
by Jae Chung, Used by permission.

This song opened the March 2003 Waterwind Asian American Worship Conference (Frederic I. Drexler Lectureship) at the American Baptist Seminary of the West, Berkeley, California. It is discussed further in Chapter 6.

```
C          G
Do you see us, O God?
Am          /G              F
Do you hear when we softly sigh?
C                      G
Do you know, we often cry?
C              G
Come now and touch, O God,
Am          /G              F
Creating in us a brand new song,
        G        C
Helping us to get along.
F          G          C          F
We know that there's no easy answer sometimes
F          G              C          C7
The pain is so much greater than what we can bear alone.
    F              G          Am
O Christ our Savior, came to suffer, loving to the cross,
F          G          C
Gave us the hope to carry on.
```

Audio version of Jae Chung's 2003 performance at Waterwind available at: www.youtube.com/watch?v=P0BciuUzmoE

SPOKEN WORD
"Asian American Characters Sketch"
by Russell Yee

Women: Readers #1, 3
Men: Readers #2, 4

Reader #1: One of the teachers of the law came and heard them debating. Noticing that Jesus had given them a good answer, he asked him, "Of all the commandments, which is the most important?"

Reader #2: "The most important one," answered Jesus, "is this: 'Hear, O Israel: The Lord our God, the Lord is one. Love the Lord your God with all your heart and with all your soul and with all your mind and with all your strength.' The second is this: 'Love your neighbor as yourself.' There is no commandment greater than these." (Mark 12:28-31, NIV)

Reader #3: I am a descendent of the first Filipino Manilamen, who sailed on a Spanish Galleon and landed in what became Louisiana.

Reader #4: I am a descendent of a Chinese railroad worker, who saw two of his kinsmen die for every three miles of track laid.

Reader #2: I am a son of an American citizen of Japanese descent, who was tagged and sent to the desert to live out the war in a tar paper shack, without guilt but so full of shame.

Reader #3: I am a Korean Christian, with relatives in North Korea who may or may not still be alive. My father gets up at 5 a.m. every day to call out our names to God.

Reader #1: I am a Filipino airport security worker and I lost my job after ten years because I'm not a U.S. citizen.

Reader #4: I am a Cambodian teenager whose family went from the Killing Fields of Pol Pot to the killing streets of American gangs. I never knew my father. My brother got arrested and then deported to Cambodia even though he doesn't even speak Khmer.

Reader #3: I am Hmong from Laos. My father worked for the CIA. He spent twelve years in a refugee camp in Thailand, which is where I was born.

Reader #1: I am Mien from Laos. My father worked for the CIA, too. When we first came to America, our people did not even have a written language.

Reader #2: I am Lao from Laos. My father didn't work for the CIA. But since the war didn't go too well, here I am.

Reader #4: I am Vietnamese but actually I'm Chinese from Vietnam. My mom was one of those boat people—you remember.

Reader #1: I am Karen from Burma, though I was actually born in Thailand. In Burma my people are a persecuted minority, so being in America now is our first taste of freedom and equality.
Reader #2: I am the son of the waitress at your neigh-

borhood Chinese take-out restaurant, where my mother works 7 days a week, 363 days a year. Last year she was held up at gunpoint only once. All this is hopefully so I can have a better life.

Reader #3: I am a student at Cal, where my parents studied after coming from Taiwan. I work so hard to honor and please them but I am so afraid of failing.

Reader #4: I am an Amerasian war child, from the American War. Even though I'm a grandparent now, I am still looking for myself.

Reader #2: I am Hapa: I am Japanese-Jewish; I am Filipino-African; I am Korean-Caucasian; I am Irish-Chinese. In 2000 I had fun filling out the U.S. Census form!

Reader #1: I'm one of those girls from China who was adopted by a Caucasian family—you know, the kind you see in children's adoption books. My parents try so hard to make sure I'm learning Chinese and Chinese culture—but is that who I really am?

Reader #4: I am a Cambodian donut shop owner.
Reader #3: I am a Vietnamese beautician.
Reader #2: I am a Chinese pharmacist.
Reader #1: I am a Filipina nurse.
Reader #3: I am Chin, from Burma.
Reader #4: I am a Korean shopkeeper.
Reader #2: I am Samoan.
Reader #1: I am Native Hawaiian.
Reader #3: I am Asian Indian.
Reader #4: I am Indo-Caribbean.
Reader #1: I am Tongan.

Reader #3: I am Guamanian. ["Gua - MAY - nee - en"]

Reader #2: I am Thai.

Reader #4: I am Singaporean—and I still chew gum.

Reader #3: I am Bangladeshi—so don't you dare call me Pakistani!

Reader #1: I am your neighbor, your classmate, your coworker, and Jesus loves me.

Reader #2: JESUS loves me!

Reader #3: Jesus LOVES me!

Reader #4: Jesus loves ME!

Reader #3: People will come from east and west and north and south, and will take their places at the feast in the kingdom of God. Indeed there are those who are last who will be first, and first who will be last." (Luke 13:29-30, NIV)

Reader #1: After this I saw a vast crowd, too great to count, from every nation and tribe and people and language, standing in front of the throne and before the Lamb. They were clothed in white and held palm branches in their hands. And they were shouting with a mighty shout, "Salvation comes from our God who sits on the throne and from the Lamb!" (Revelation 7:9-10, NLT)

ALL (shouting): I am Asian American—and Jesus loves me!

See "Asian American Characters Sketch," from the Calvin Worship Renewal Grants regional gathering, November 1, 2008, in Pleasant Hill, California, at www.youtube.com/watch?v=SSKiAXJyh3Y

SPOKEN WORD
"Freedom (A Psalm)"
by Ron Chin
Used by permission

Show me a new way, God
    Lead me to your freedom and grace
Let me see your goodness
    I desire to gaze into your face

Everywhere I travel
    Into every place I step foot
The fear of losing face follows me
    The Pharaoh of my soul pursues me
I am like the Golden Gate
    Chilled by the fog
Like the San Andreas
    Quivering like a quake

I do what people want
    I hardly ever make mistakes
But an emptiness fills me
    It grips me deep inside
Where is the real me?
    Do I have a true self?
It's buried in me somewhere
    Deep down within me
    Beneath this compliant face

Lord, you are my creator
    You are the maker of great works
You look at me with an approving eye

You have a smile on your face
You tell me you love me
that I am of great worth
I want to deeply know these truths
I receive your Spirit in my heart
So I can walk in freedom
Being whom you made me
Living in your unfailing grace

SPOKEN WORD
"A Voice from the True North"
By Rita Chang
Used by permission

I arrived in the '70s from Hong Kong to Toronto
From a crowded place to open space
I started with Mandarin and Cantonese
And ended up with English and French,
    plus an "eh?" to end every sentence—eh?
I am from Air Canada and Petro Canada
French fries with gravy, Tim Hortons and Swiss Chalet
I'm from beef chow fun
    and all kinds of Hong Kong–style noodles
Jasmine tea to milk tea
I'm from colorful paper money with a
    purse full of loonies and toonies
From regular sales tax to now PST + GST
I am from Mississauga, a suburb west of Toronto
Transits, subways, highways 427, 401, and QEW
I am from the four changing seasons
Blooming flowers, high humidity,
    falling colorful maple leaves, and icy blizzards
I'm from CFL Football, Hockey Night in Canada,
    SCTV
From Wayne Gretzky, Anne Murray,
    Celine Dion, John Candy, and Mike Myers
I'm from a small Baptist church plant
Where our English service was held in a side room with
    mostly youth
I'm from an immigrant family,
    hard-working and longsuffering

Meeting my husband and his family,
    who are American-born Chinese, carefree
    and educated
I'm now American, Canadian, Hong Kong, Shandong
From homemade dumplings and noodles, and garden
    grown vegetables
I'm a follower of Jesus, blessed wife of Pastor Harrison
    and mother to Matthew and Lauren
Loved by God and saved by his wonderful grace

SPOKEN WORD
"My Cultural-Religious Identity"
By Russell Jeung
Used by permission.

I'm a Jeung
I am from the televised '70s
From Fritos and the 49ers
I am from the San Francisco Richmond
Foghorns, seal barks, and the 38 Geary
I am from eucalyptus, iceplants, and redwoods
Towering in steep, fern-lined ravines
I'm from Sunday Chinese dinners and ocean cruises
From Bobo and Jeung Sam Mui
I'm from the cheeky
And the droll
From "draw the drapes" and
"you're gonna to go to boarding school if you
        don't behave..."
I'm from a Bible church
Where we had jook after Christmas caroling
I'm from San Francisco and Zhongshan
Crab and roast pork for Thanksgiving
From the great-grandfather who fished in Monterey
The mother who raised ten kids besides her own
12th Avenue, Stanyan Street, Oak Park, Murder Dubs
I'm from the working class and the academy
Husband of Joan, Daddy of Matthew, Foster Parent
        of Bethsy and Bonny
Child of God

SPOKEN WORD
"The Gospel and My People"
by Nhuanh Ly
Used by permission.

I am a second-generation Vietnamese American.
Born and raised in Little Saigon,
a little area of Orange County where more Vietnamese
    gone
to gather and make ourselves a home
away from home. A home away from home.

I am from a people who eat nước mắm
and aren't afraid of fishy breath.
A people who say *"Anh ơi," "Dạ,"* and *"Nước sôi,*
    nước sôi!"
I am from a people who celebrate Tết
with firecrackers, bánh chưng, and red envelopes.
Who greet everyone differently depending on their age,
gender, and relationship to us.

I am from a people who fear that our lives
here in America would be worse
than our lives back in Vietnam.
So we work hard, work hard to make sure
that we make it better.

I am from a people who wear white to funerals
and have rituals every 7, 49, 100, and 365 days
to send off our loved ones' souls.
Who wouldn't let me cry when I saw my daddy's spirit
go on day 1.

I am from a people who put their hope
in a fellow
with long earlobes,
and a jumbo
belly.

I am from a family who used to think that Jesus was
     a white version of Buddha
and believed that all religions help you achieve life
     after death.
I am from a family who first heard about Jesus
when a small red brick Baptist church in
     Louisville, Kentucky
sponsored my mommy and daddy to nước Mỹ.
And a second time, when a Chinese American woman
spoke about Jesus in her broken English
while my stepdad listened, filtering out the words he
     didn't know,
and soaking in the limited vocabulary he could follow:
     "truth," "save," "love."

When I was growing up, the Vietnamese Christian
     & Missionary Alliance
was so small that we would all get together
every winter, spring, summer, and fall
for sports tournaments and camps.
I knew all of them.
I thought I wasn't missin' any Vietnamese
     American Christian.

When I was growing up, my mom spoke of Christianity
as a spirituality that we are privileged to have found,
since in Communist Vietnam, to speak of Jesus, you'd
go down.

My dad spoke of Christianity as a white man's religion,
one that assumes assimilation
if one becomes born once again.

Today, I thank God that my daddy is now,
not assimilated to white American culture,
but assimilated to the Kingdom culture
of the Most High.

I am from a people who need to hear,
who need to hear about Christ's
truth, salvation, and love.

Jesus, I pray for all the Vietnamese here in America,
all the Vietnamese back at home,
that by your grace, we will all be saturated with your
truth, salvation, and love.
Amen.

Video of Nhuanh Ly performing her piece at the 2008 convention of the Hymn Society in the United States and Canada, meeting at First Presbyterian Church of Berkeley: "Nhuanh @ Hymn Society 2008," www.you tube.com/watch?v=crDjaicHeyM

SPOKEN WORD AND PSALM WRITING
Three Templates

Spoken word is a contemporary form of public poetry reading. It's less fully rhythmic than rap music but, like rap, does not depend on musical tonality. As in poetry, the greater part of the meaning comes from precise word choice and phrasing. Spoken word works well for public readings, typically much better than, say, straight essay readings. The thoughts are pithy and evocative, and the pieces tend to be relatively brief.

One way to help and to motivate people to write and share spoken word pieces is to first give them a template they can follow. If you just give people a blank piece of paper, or even a blank piece of paper and a topic ("Your Spiritual Journey"), it's quite a challenge to write something they would be ready to share. But if you give people a template—say a list of ten or twelve specific descriptive prompts—it becomes very much easier to write and share a complete piece. Indeed, if you give several people the same template, they can share their completed pieces back to back for added insight, delight, and effect.

Following are two spoken word templates, on which the previous two spoken word pieces were based, and a third template for a modern psalm. Try coming up with your own pieces based on these templates, or even create your own templates.

My Cultural-Religious Identity
[template]

1. I am from (childhood cultural touchstone)
   From (product name) and (anything)
2. I am from the (home description)
   (adjective, adjective, sensory details)
3. I am from the (plant, flower, natural item)
   The (plant, flower, natural item)
4. I'm from (family tradition) and (family trait)
   From (name of family member) and (another name
   of family member)
5. I'm from the (description of family tendency)
   And (another family tendency)
6. From (something you were told as a child) and
   (something else you were told as a child)
7. I'm from (representation of religion or lack of it)
   (further description)
8. I'm from (place of birth and family ancestry)
   (two food items representing your family)
9. From the (family story about a specific person and a detail)
   The (another detail of family member)
10. (List locations of family pictures, mementos, archives)
11. I am from (several more lines indicating what makes
    you unique)

The Gospel and My People
[template]

1. I'm from [place of birth and family ancestry]
2. a people who [two happy and beautiful cultural gifts]
a people who say [some well-known phrases]
3. I'm from a people who celebrate [one or more annual holidays/festivals/remembrances] and who [some cultural customs or practices].
4. I'm from a people who put their hopes in [a particular deity, religious belief, and/or practice] and who feared [very bad things that one could do or that could happen to the family].
5. I'm from a people who [funeral/burial customs and any ongoing attention to those who have passed away].
6. I'm from a people who greatly value [things that were directly or indirectly held up as most important].
7. I'm from a people/family who first heard about Jesus when [specific place/time/setting/language/event/people] and who (probably) first thought that Jesus was [ideas you might guess].
8. When I was growing up, church was [whatever it was] and my parents spoke of Christians as [whatever they said, if anything].
9. Now today [anything about churches and Christians among your people].
10. I'm from a people who need to hear [some aspect of the Christian gospel that particularly speaks to the needs of your people].
11. Jesus, I pray for [how you describe your family's people], that by your grace [one or two specific requests]. Amen.

Psalm Writing
[template]

The most basic structure of Hebrew poetry is not rhyme but par-allelism—saying things twice in a row in a slightly different way. Here is a template for writing a psalm of lament.

1. Describe God in a way that would specially help you right now.
Lord, you are the one who _____
The one who _____
2. Complain about something you care about and want God to show more care about (two parallel lines).
3. Ask God for something specific (two parallel lines).
4. Give God a good reason to answer your request. Be fearless! (two parallel lines)
5. Recall a time in the past when God came through for you (two parallel lines).
6. Express confidence in God's goodness and care (two parallel lines).

ASIAN POETRY FORMS

The cultures of Asia offer a rich variety of short poetic forms that may be integrated powerfully in written worship materials or as spoken word pieces and individual or congregational prayers. Here are basic descriptions of just a few.

Haiku (Japan)

Generally, the haiku is composed of three metrical lines of five, seven, and five syllables, respectively. The poet "cuts" the three units into two parts, creating an imaginative distance between the two parts. The parts will remain independent of each other (often reflected in English with punctuation, such as a colon [:], em-dash [—], or ellipsis [...]), but one will enrich the reader's understanding of the other. While some suggest that the subject matter traditionally refers to nature, a wide variety of topics can be found in Japanese and English haiku. Convention does, however, insist that all haiku include a "season word" (*kigo*), which establishes directly or implicitly the seasonal context of the poem (e.g., snowflake, cherry blossom). Haiku traditionally strives for objectivity over flowery metaphor, but it also thrives on clever wordplays, allusions, and puns. Because haiku is so short and deceptively simple, it may work best in a printed form for reflection and meditation.

(Sources: www.toyomasu.com/haiku and http://thewordshop .tripod.com/Sijo/sijo-index.htm, accessed October 6, 2011.)

Tanka (Japan)

Traced back to poetry contests of the twelfth century, the classic tanka contains 31 sound-symbols (*onji*). *Onji* are the smallest linguistic unit in Japanese poetry, and although they don't really correspond to syllables in English, early translators determined that English tanka would consist of 31 syllables. Traditionally, this takes the form of five lines of 5-7-5-7-7 syllables, although variations on this are frequent. (Five lines of 2-3-2-3-3 syllables is probably closer to the Japanese intent.) The subject matter of tanka usually involves intense personal feelings, often contrasting these emotions with natural phenomena, including changing seasons. Thus, tanka is considered a more subjective and metaphoric form of poetry than haiku. And while tanka does not rhyme, it does make wonderful use of sound, including alliteration (same-sound initial consonants, e.g., "lovely lotus"), assonance (similar internal sounds, e.g., "shining light guides"), onomatopoeia (words that imitate sound, e.g., "hum" or "sizzle"), and even some repetition. Thus it lends itself to spoken word or congregational prayer.

(Source: http://thewordshop.tripod.com/asian/Japan/tankadef .html, accessed October 6, 2011.)

Sijo (Korea)

Originally called tanga, meaning "short song," the sijo was (and often still is) set to music. It resembles the haiku inasmuch as it is traditionally set in three lines and often takes nature for its subject matter. However, unlike its Japanese cousin, sijo has longer lines (between 14–16 syllables each, for a total of 44–46 syllables) and it may be narrative as well as thematic. Indeed, sijo is distinctive in that line one establishes a problem or situation, line 2 introduces a development or *turn*, and line 3 begins with a *twist* that ultimately resolves the tension or question in a memorable ending. Because each of the three lines is marked by an internal pause, some English writers and translators format the sijo in six shorter lines instead of the traditional three long lines. Like the tanka, sijo often employs metaphor and other figurative language, but it also relies on wordplay and puns, like the haiku.

(Source: http://thewordshop.tripod.com/Sijo/sijo-index.htm, accessed October 6, 2011.)

Climbing Rhyme (Burma)

Poetry in Burma has a long and notable history, and it comes in a variety of classical forms. However, most forms are distinguished by a pattern called the climbing rhyme—where three lines of four syllables apiece feature a repeated sequence of internal rhymes. This contrasts traditional English end rhyme, where the final syllable of two or more lines will rhyme in a variety of patterns (A-B-B-A, or A-B-A-B, or A-B-C-B). In a climbing rhyme, the rhyme occurs in line one–syllable 4, line two–syllable 3, and line three–syllable 2 (the 4-3-2 scheme), forming a stair-step that is renewed in the final syllable of line three to create a new 4-3-2 pattern. This form is particularly effective in the Burmese language, which is essentially monosyllabic (i.e., each syllable has meaning, so four syllables are often four words). If creating a climbing rhyme in English, then it might be more effective to create the internal rhymes using four words, rather than four syllables, per line. It may be less metrical than the original form, but it presents the opportunity to create sound harmonies that appeal to lovers of rhyme without the sing-song bounce disliked by those who prefer prose or free verse. The result is both tightly structured but with a feel of freedom and variety, useful in print or spoken aloud.

(Source: http://thewordshop.tripod.com/asian/climbingrhyme .htm, accessed October 6, 2011.)

IDEAS FOR PROJECTED IMAGES

The widespread use of projected images during worship services opens up many opportunities for contextualization in worship. Images of pretty sunsets, waterfalls, and mountains are inspiring depictions of God's handiwork in creation, but are very generic. What if your images included some of the following?

❖ *ANA faces*
❖ *ANA places (local, regional, national, international)*
❖ *Words in ANA ancestral languages*
❖ *Images from ANA-related current new events*
❖ *cons or other depictions of biblical characters and scenes in an Asian style (a Korean nativity, a Vietnamese depiction of Jesus in the boat calming the storm, a Chinese depiction of the feeding of the five thousand)*
❖ *Images from your church's actual, physical neighborhood, and your church's city. We make a specialty of this at New Hope Covenant Church in Oakland, including images that are not particularly pretty but that depict the very place we feel called to live in and serve.*

Worship Stations

Worship stations are focused, interactive settings within the Sunday worship space where people can pray about and reflect upon specific themes and topics. Worship stations tend to emphasize visual and tactile creativity and invite some kind of interactive response.

At New Hope Covenant Church in Oakland, California, our practice is to provide worship stations once a month (although we have weekly Communion—which is the central worship station of Christian worship). A segment of the worship service is given to the worship stations, and during that time, worshippers are invited to visit the several worship stations set up around the perimeter of our worship space, this with background music playing, and with Communion provided at a self-serve worship station in the center. We let go of the idea that we all need to be doing the same thing at the same time as directed from the front. Even though most of the interaction is self-directed, there is always an intense sense of shared prayer and worship. In our particular setting, many stations are often arranged with carpets on the floor, so that kneeling and sitting provide ready and active ways to express our prayers and worship intentions. Also, if you give people a way to write brief prayers (say, on a poster board, or on sticky notes, or on a white board) then others can also read and offer up those prayers.

You can also create a culture in which people freely interact with the worship stations throughout the service—there is no expectation that to be a good worshipper you must, say, sit and listen quietly to the sermon from beginning to end. This can be especially helpful for children and youth who stay in the service. Why should we teach them that worship is mostly sitting quietly? At times we have experimented with a "Kidz Zone" right near the front of our worship space: some carpets with building blocks and coloring pads, supervised by one or two adults. (It's up front because we figure we can't expect kids to be interested in worship if they can't see what is going on.) Once, one of our children was building quite a structure with blocks, and after the service he told his mom, "I was building God's house."

Worship stations work especially well for those with more introverted, reflective personalities. It gives people the opportunity for active expression without requiring or forcing that expression, and especially not requiring openly verbal and directly interpersonal expression. So much of contemporary, western worship is biased towards extroverted personalities. The heavy

*dependence on praise music, which privileges audible expression
and cued gesture, does not work for everyone, and especially not
for those who are more reserved.*

*Worship stations are certainly nothing new. In Eastern
Orthodox and also Roman Catholic worship there has been a
very long tradition of side altars and side chapels within churches, often inviting worshippers to light candles, kneel, and pray.
There has also been the longstanding use of Stations of the Cross
(following Jesus' Passion with a specific devotional path using
fourteen or so images of specific scenes from his suffering, death,
and burial). Of course, this has involved the use of icons, relics,
and saints in ways that have been matters of huge theological
controversies, especially during the Reformation. But the essential idea—that individual silent prayer can be part of shared
devotion—is precisely the same.*

*Following I've provided some worship station ideas. All it
takes is just a few simple objects or images, some simple signage,
and some pens and slips of paper or sticky notes to write out
prayers. Or one can get more elaborate, using laptop computers
or digital picture frames, audio clip players, and so forth. There
is surely plenty of untapped creativity for such things among the
youth and adults at your church right now.*

Worship Station #1:
Confession

A simple cross and either blank slips of paper and pens or an assortment of preprinted individual and/or societal sins for people to place at the cross. Works well on a rug on the floor.

Prayers for the World/Prayers for My World

Maps of the world, maps of your church's immediate neighborhood, flags, pictures of your church and of your church's missionaries, relevant newspaper and magazine headlines and such. We had a station for the 2008 Beijing Olympics.

Prayers for Women

The Mid-Autumn Moon Festival (celebrated in Chinese, Korean, and Vietnamese cultures) is especially associated with women because the moon is considered "*yin*" (versus the male "*yang*" of the sun). This midpoint between seasons (late October early November) can be an occasion for prayers for girls and women, perhaps emphasizing ANA-related issues (e.g., persistent male bias in places like China).

Other Cultural Customs and Celebrations

How about a Chinese red egg and ginger station for baby Jesus? A Japanese cherry blossom festival for the rebirth of Easter? A Vietnamese *Tết* station with traditional new year's flowers (*hoa mai, hoa đào*) and prayers for families?

Other ideas:

❖ Prayers for Students and your Local Schools
❖ Prayers for Elections (around election time)
❖ Prayers for Social Justice (what are the actual live issues in your community and city?)

❖ Prayers for Driving (when's the last time you prayed about your driving?)
❖ Prayers for the Environment
❖ Prayers for Families and Relatives
❖ Prayers for Government Leaders
❖ Prayers for Current Events
❖ Prayers for Addictions, Resentments, etc.
❖ Prayers for our Finances

Video of worship stations in action at New Hope Covenant Church, Oakland, July 20, 2008: www.youtube.com/watch?v=6hdd9SVktko

Many other churches have uploaded such videos; search for "prayer stations" and "worship stations."

Worship Station #2:
Communion Prayers

The prayer of consecration over the food and drink of the Lord's Table is a prime opportunity for cultural contextualization.

One approach is to write the prayer using a Trinitarian form that dates back to the early church:

1. *Thanksgiving to God the Father for acts of creation (here include references to specific people groups, their journeys and gifts).* "Holy and gracious God, we thank you for creating the heavens and the earth, and all peoples, with all their languages and histories, including our own ancestors in Asia and in Europe, and the journeys that led to our presence here..."

2. *Remembrance of God the Son for acts of redemption (here include the institution narrative from 1 Corinthians 11:23-25 and adding references to specific trials [e.g., survival from wartime suffering] and sins [e.g., model minority pridefulness and self-sufficiency]).* "On the night he was betrayed, he took bread....Jesus, we ask that your blood would cover the shame we still carry from our peoples' sufferings and deprivations, from our names and our accents, and from comparing ourselves to other peoples in envy or in spite..."

3. *Invocation/invitation to God the Holy Spirit to bless and consecrate this particular food and drink for Communion, and these particular people who come to partake (here include references to your church's particular place and calling).* "Holy Spirit, set us apart along with this food and this cup, as holy gifts for holy people. Nourish us to reach our kinsfolk, to bring healing to our own community and to this neighborhood, and to help us understand each other across our different generations…"

Try asking some of your youth to write a prayer for Communion. When the time for consecration comes, you can be sure they will be listening. Ask them to write other prayers for worship as well, perhaps adapting a Psalm, or the Beatitudes, or the Lord's Prayer by adding references to their own lives and world.

Conclusion

I once heard a professional Asian American jazz musician say that when he plays with other Asian American musicians, so often the concern is to play the music *right*. In contrast, he said that when he plays with African American musicians, "We just *breathe together*." At the end of Psalm 150, it says, "Let everything that breathes praise the LORD!" Sometimes I think ANA worship leaders need to learn to simply relax and breathe. Now that I have written this book and you have read it, let's just relax and breathe. And then let us continue worshipping on the Way.

The early church had a saying: *lex orandi, lex credendi,* "the law of worship [is] the law of belief." As the church developed its early creeds it looked to its worship life as the foundation for what would become its doctrines. (For instance, worshipping Jesus helped the early church come to its understanding of Jesus' divinity.) But we can apply this saying another way: what does our worship say about what we believe? Specifically, what does the worship in our ANA church settings say about our beliefs concerning matters of culture and identity? Would we conclude from observing our worship that we believe "west is best" (whether or not we would say it that way), or that biculturality is optional, or that ancestry matters only when it's a problem? Too often I'm afraid our "law of worship" would readily give evidence for such beliefs. This book has been an attempt to bring the process full circle by adding *lex credendi, lex orandi,* "let's examine and reconsider some of our beliefs about matters of culture and identity, and then see how that might affect how we design and lead our worship."

230

I have (hopefully) made your life more interesting (actually, more complicated) by raising diverse questions about worship in ANA settings and touching upon the cultural work that lies before us in shaping and ordering worship. I hope I've persuaded you that Scripture allows and even requires creativity in our worship lives. I hope I've convinced you that this requires us to fully engage and embrace matters of culture. I hope I've portrayed a good and beautiful place called Asian North America, a place that it is culturally young and still, like a teenager, in the process of finding itself. I hope I've offered enough guidelines and strategies to make experimentation worth the risks involved. And I hope I've inspired you with a few expressions of ANA worship.

My hope is that within another generation or so, someone else will have occasion to write a book on this same topic, but filled with manifold examples of ANA worship that have since blossomed, deeper and better questions about culture and faith, and beautiful stories of how ANA churches have well served the wider church in North America and worldwide.

Some years ago I was helping a local ANA church decide whether it would promote itself as Asian American, or whether it would develop in a more multicultural direction. Then a member reminded the group that its own origins were in a bilingual church where the English-speaking and Chinese-speaking ministries had parted ways. "We can't even get along with other Chinese," she observed, "so how are we supposed to get along with *everyone*?" Of course, sometimes it's hardest to get along with those closest to us, but her point stands. The only way to reach *every*one is for *each* of our churches to reach *someone*. And for a good many ANA believers, that someone is other ANAs. Is anyone else better qualified or positioned to reach ANAs? And is anyone else going to cultivate an intentionally ANA voice and presence in worship? "I have great sorrow and unceasing anguish in my heart. For I could wish that I myself were accursed and cut off from Christ for the sake of my own people, my kindred according to the flesh" (Romans 9:2-3).

The Christian journey revolves around two centers: Jesus' cross and his empty tomb. The cross is about relinquishing and dying to self. The tomb is about resurrecting and embracing new life. Author Eric Law makes the point that we are always in the process of moving from one center to the other. When we are in a place of established strength, we need to set our eyes on the cross and learn to let go. When we are in a place of weakness and emptiness, we need to focus on the empty tomb and learn to grow in new life and strength. Generally speaking I believe that majority-culture worship needs movement toward the cross, while ANA worship needs movement toward the empty tomb. I hope this book inspires movement toward new life.

Protestants like me have no formal church hierarchy to give us authoritative direction about such things. Can we give each other permission to explore and experiment with cultural expressions of worship? Can we invite and suggest more than we critique and question? Can we resist signaling disapproval, and look instead for opportunities to encourage and help? The last thing we need is more fear of failure, let alone fear of judgment or dismissal.

This is not to say "anything goes" or that we don't need strong, responsible discernment. I myself believe we need to stay within the horizon of Scripture itself and to remain absolutely and exclusively loyal to the one who said, "I am the way, and the truth, and the life" (John 14:6). It is out of such loyalty that I want to press further into ANA worship because I am convinced there are parts of Jesus we will not get to know or enjoy if we do not find him in the very culture and identity he gave us. And that would be to rob him, rob us, and rob the wider church.

"Now to him who by the power at work within us is able to accomplish abundantly far more than all we can ask or imagine, to him be glory in the church and in Christ Jesus to all generations, forever and ever. Amen" (Ephesians 3:20-21). Surely this is a lot to ask for and to imagine: a full and thriving ANA worship movement, expressed in many different forms and settings, and vitally connected with life-giving developments in ANA discipleship, spirituality, evangelism, and social action. Yet God promises even more than that, more than I can imagine for you in these pages.

Lord Jesus, give us the faith to believe your promises are true for us, your ANA followers. Show us that becoming more and more ANA can be our way of becoming more and more like you. Give us the courage to offer back to you all of who and what you made us. Amen.

> I saw no temple in the city, for its temple is the Lord God the Almighty and the Lamb. And the city has no need of sun or moon to shine on it, for the glory of God is its light, and its lamp is the Lamb. The nations will walk by its light, and the kings of the earth will bring their glory into it. Its gates will never be shut by day—and there will be no night there. People will bring into it the glory and the honor of the nations. (Revelation 21:22-26)

Author's Contact Information
E-mail: worshipontheway@gmail.com
Blog: www.worshipontheway.blogspot.com

Look for more at:
www.worshipontheway.blogspot.com

❖ All the links mentioned in the book

❖ Annotated pictures, videos, and audio from worship settings

❖ Links to other worship and culture websites

❖ Notes on other books and articles of interest

❖ Downloadable materials

❖ Reviews of *Worship on the Way*

❖ Reader contributions

❖ Russell Yee's ongoing thoughts about *Worship on the Way*

❖ News and upcoming events with Russell Yee

❖ Recommended resources